The Old Testament in 48 Hours

The Old Testament in 48 Hours

KEITH BODNER

CASCADE *Books* • Eugene, Oregon

THE OLD TESTAMENT IN 48 HOURS

Cascade Books
An Imprint of Wipf and Stock Publishers
199 W. 8th Ave., Suite 3
Eugene, OR 97401

www.wipfandstock.com

PAPERBACK ISBN: 979-8-3852-3681-7
HARDCOVER ISBN: 979-8-3852-3682-4
EBOOK ISBN: 979-8-3852-3683-1

Cataloguing-in-Publication data:

Names: Bodner, Keith | author.

Title: The Old Testament in 48 Hours

Description: Eugene, OR: Cascade Books, 2025

Identifiers: ISBN 979-8-3852-3681-7 (paperback) | ISBN 979-8-3852-3682-4 (hardcover) | ISBN 979-8-3852-3683-1 (ebook)

Subjects: LCSH: Bible Old Testament—Criticism, interpretation, etc. | Bible—Study and teaching

Classification: BS1171.3 B63 2026 (paperback) | BS1171.3 (ebook)

02/27/26

Contents

Introduction

How is it possible that such an old book can still be on the bestseller lists? Defying the odds, the Bible has a global reach and remains the most influential work in the history of publishing, casting its shadow on other literature, art, music, and cinema. The Bible even remains a part of standard college courses today—alongside Chaucer, Dante, Milton, Shakespeare, Tolstoy, Jane Austen, Kierkegaard, and the Brontë sisters—and continues to generate vigorous debate and discussion.

Yet the experience of many who arrive at the Bible for the first time, whether out of necessity or by sheer curiosity, is a healthy sense of shock. Perhaps they were expecting to find a random assortment of pious platitudes or boring religiosity. But what these readers actually encounter is a strange, yet familiar world of human drama and struggle, replete with tragedy and humor, in both rustic settings and against the backdrop of empires. A remarkable variety of literary genres are found in the Bible, ranging from narrative prose and legal discourse, all the way to poetic lyrics and apocalyptic unveilings. Despite such diversity within the many different books of the Bible, there is nonetheless an overarching storyline that can be read from start to finish.

Some obstacles, however, can be found along the way. In teaching the Bible for the past three decades I've noticed that quite a few students struggle with the Old Testament material, and so our goal is to overcome this hurdle. This book is directed to any reader who is trying to make sense of the deceptions of Jacob and the suffering of Job, the career of Jeremiah and keeping track of dozens of Zechariahs, not to mention figuring out sacrifices and sanctuaries, priests and prophets, kings and pharaohs, and the frequent attacks of Assyrians, Ammonites, Amalekites, Arameans, Hittites, Hivites, Cellulites, and whomever else. Our aim is to efficiently survey the entire contents of the Old Testament, with a focus on the major contours of the plot, the central characters, and some of the overall themes that emerge. By getting through the Old Testament, readers are then much better prepared to appreciate the New Testament.

In terms of organization, this book will follow the traditional Jewish ordering for the Hebrew Bible/Old Testament material: the **Law**, the **Prophets**, and the **Writings**.

- The **Law**, or *Torah*, is compromised of the first five books (Genesis to Deuteronomy, usually called the Pentateuch) and unfolds the story from creation and the flood, through the promise to Abraham and the people of Israel, as well as the exodus from Egypt and the journey in the wilderness until they reach the edge of the promised land.
- The **Prophets** are divided into two sections: the Former Prophets (Joshua to 2 Kings) traces Israel's experience in the land from entrance until exile, while the Later Prophets (Isaiah, Jeremiah, Ezekiel, and the book of the Twelve) present the oracles and poetry from the great voices of the prophetic past.
- The **Writings** include Israel's wisdom literature (Psalms, Job, Proverbs), the five festal scrolls (Ruth to Esther), Daniel, and the concluding historical books of Ezra and Nehemiah, along with 1 and 2 Chronicles.

Those readers who have a version of the Bible such as the King James, the New International Version, or the New Revised Standard Version will notice a different ordering the books in the table of contents. Here the books are arranged in a more chronological sequence, rather than a topical or thematic grouping. But either way, it is not that difficult to make the adjustment: the same thirty-nine books are simply arranged in a different sequences. Of course, it provides a slightly different experience to read Job after the book of Psalms, or to read 2 Chronicles as the last book rather than Malachi. The different ordering of the books, therefore, provide new ways to appreciate the larger story.

Overall, this short book is designed as a guidebook to accompany the journey of reading the Old Testament/Hebrew Bible, and is certainly not a substitute for reading the Bible itself. Instead, it is meant to be consulted alongside the biblical text, and it will be assumed that an opened Bible will be close at hand. Furthermore, this book does not provide any rigorous defense of the biblical text, nor present any case for faith or address some of our more pressing ethical questions. Instead, you will find here a few words of overview designed to help you get started, and encourage a complete reading of these thirty-nine books. You will also get a bit of help to overcome some of the hurdles that often prevent us from reaching through the finish line.

Similarly, there will be lots of exciting matters that won't be addressed. For example, there is no discussion about the fact that the Bible has hundreds of authors and contributors, working in several languages over many centuries in more than one country. There are no maps or pictures, and no lengthy historical digressions about Babylonian calendars or Sumerian ziggurats. There aren't any archaeological trips to visit the stele of Merneptah (the oldest mention of Israel outside the Bible discovered to this point, ~1200 BCE) or the Moabite Stone (providing insight on King Mesha and the worship of the god Chemosh, helpful background for 2 Kings 3). There will not be enough time to compare the book of Proverbs with the Egyptian Instruction of Amenemope, nor any comparison between the birth narratives of Sargon and Moses.

As a modest attempt to compensate for such shortcomings, there is a brief list "for further reading" at the end. These various resources are suggested in order to assist anyone interested in deepening their study. This list includes translations, an atlas, and reference works, as well as studies that delve into historical background and useful commentaries. Anyone interested in probing a date of composition for the earliest lyrics or theories about later editing during the post-exilic period is referred to this further reading. Unless otherwise indicated, translations are my own, and sometimes verge on paraphrase in order to convey the sense of immediacy in a particular scene. It is hoped that readers from different religious traditions (or none at all) will find a respectful discussion in these pages that honors the text—even in its darker turns—while providing a user-friendly summary. Of course, the various topics covered here (and omitted) will certainly not be to everyone's satisfaction. So, if any of my scholarly colleagues are disappointed, I have to appeal to the words of Yoda: *written for you this book was not.*

At a period in our contemporary world when study of the Bible is becoming more diverse and more interesting than ever, this short book aims to unfold the Old Testament story for a fresh set of readers. Altogether the compelling plots of biblical stories and the extraordinary cast of characters have an abiding entertainment value and are a surprising repository of wisdom. Seldom does a day go by when some biblical turn of phrase is not echoed, whether *the writing on the wall*, *David versus Goliath*, *love your neighbor as yourself*, and even the fearful beast *Leviathan* is the name of one of the world's tallest roller coasters. The plan is to start slowly, lingering over the early chapters of Genesis, but then pick up the pace as we generate some momentum. At the end of this book we will notice that much more has been left out than included, and our exploration here is only the beginning. And speaking of *in the beginning*, it is now time to get going.

Hour 1: Genesis 1–2

For the reader coming to the Bible from other classics, the beginning of Genesis is unique. Homer's *Iliad*, we recall, starts in the middle of the story, with the Greeks on a beach and the two greatest figures—Achilles the warrior and Agamemnon the ruler—engaged in a quarrel. By contrast, Genesis seemingly begins prior to the creation of time. The first sentence of Genesis might sound familiar to many of us, but the concept of a single God creating the universe would carry a radical edge in the ancient world, as would the next line:

> *Now the earth was vacuous and void, with darkness over the face of the deep, But God's spirit was hovering over face of the waters.*

The early chapters of Genesis can be interpreted as an overture to the entire biblical story. Creation is not a static, one-time event. God will continually be turning chaos into order, just as the dark waters of the deep are confronted with the divine spirit that is poised and ready to be activated. As the first few days unfold, a picture emerges of God as a kingly figure, a presiding magistrate who speaks a word and it is immediately implemented: from light to dry ground, and from gathered seas to growing vegetation, as the world that was once a formless waste now bursts with life. The earth itself is endowed with a latent ability, so it would seem, to regenerate (*Let the earth shoot forth plant life*), suggesting a vast ecosystem divinely designed to grow and multiply.

Such dazzling growth, however, gives rise to a potential problem on the fourth day when God makes a *greater* and a *lesser* light. The sun and the moon were worshipped as deities in many cultures, and so rather than naming them here, they are only described in terms of their illuminating functions. But how is there flourishing plant life on the previous day without these celestial objects? Evidently there are other sources of light, and so any kind of solar worship would need to be reconsidered. Similarly, on the fifth day the waters are teeming with living creatures, and God also creates the sea monsters. Elsewhere in the Bible these are terrifying dragons (e.g., Isaiah 27:1; 51:9), but here they just another element of marine life and drained of any supernatural threat. In Genesis 1 God does not have any obvious rival or serious competitor.

The apex of this eventful week, and maybe even its goal, is the creation of humanity in the divine image. To this point in the story God is someone who speaks, and uses words for life-giving purposes. Being created in God's image, then, might mean that human beings are endowed with the capacity to use words in good and beneficial ways, as well as experience relational intimacy with God. In other creation epics of the ancient Near East, humanity is often an afterthought or merely slaves for the gods. But in Genesis 1 there is a divine imprint with royal status, signaling the importance of the human person and a corresponding responsibility that is endowed.

If the opening chapter gives a big-picture perspective—cosmic drone footage, as it were, culminating with celebratory rest on the seventh day—then Genesis 2 is much closer to a ground-level point of view. In chapter 1 God speaks humanity into existence, whereas in the next chapter human beings are handcrafted with an individual touch. Indeed, the title *Lord God* is used here, combining "God" as universal creator with "Lord" (Yhwh, see Exodus 3), the exclusive name that later in the story relates to covenant partnership and faithful care.

Special status is confirmed when humanity is placed in the garden of Eden ("delightful"), associated with the world's great rivers. The reason a human being is put in the garden is to cultivate and protect it, underscoring a kind of stewardship over creation. Such a role is enhanced by naming the various animals, which implies studying and understanding the garden's vibrant biodiversity. Amidst the blossoming trees that are pleasant to the eye and ripe to eat, particular emphasis falls on two trees, first specified in v. 9, but soon the subject of a key utterance:

> *Then the Lord God commanded the man, saying: "From every tree of the garden you can most certainly eat! But from the tree of the knowledge of good and evil you cannot eat, for on the day that you eat from it, you will most certainly die."* (Genesis 2:14)

This divine speech begins with an expansive invitation to enjoy fresh fruit, and there is no reason to suspect that the tree of life is not included. Only one tree is off limits, and that tree ominously includes the term *evil.*

Seven times in chapter 1 the term *good* is used. But only now is *evil* used, in the context of going against God's word. It is worth mentioning that the Israelites will have a similar opportunity later in the story. If they listen to God's counsel they will enjoy the fruit of the promised land, but if they turn aside from it, they risk catastrophe. The two trees can be interpreted several different ways. Perhaps they represent two different pathways or options, and at this point pose the question of whether or not humanity will pay attention to the divine word, or be drawn toward the realm of evil. Either way, both trees loom large in the next chapter of Genesis.

Meanwhile, the mammoth task of naming every animal and cultivating the garden is quite a burden for a solitary Adam ("dirt"). God therefore determines to secure a fitting helper, although that English word is not quite right. If you are drowning or wounded on the battlefield, you need someone to undertake a rescue operation. That is the definition of a *helper* in the Bible (e.g., Psalm 20:1–2). The closing moments of the chapter indicate that the man and woman belong together, declaring an equality and a bond that is more durable than any kinship or contract. The man and woman are *not ashamed*, so perhaps the idea is that shame is never a factor when there is harmony with divine instruction. Ominously, a mysterious new character appears on the garden stage in the next scene and plants a seed of doubt about the reliability God's word.

Hour 2: Genesis 3–4

WITH GOD SEEMINGLY OFFSTAGE at the beginning of Genesis 3, it is probably not an accident that a clever snake assumes a central role, and starts a conversation by asking the woman a question. There is no indication that they have conversed before, and in response to the snake's inquiry (*Did God really say?*) the woman partially repeats the command about the tree of knowledge, but also intensifies it by adding that they *must not touch it*. Since God gave the command to the man, the likely explanation is that he in turn passed it on to her, but it is not clear who added the "touch" prohibition, nor why she feels compelled to include it.

The shrewdness of the snake is evident as he draws attention to something the man and woman lack, and entices them to desire it. A sinister motive can be suspected on the basis of the snake's flat contradiction: *you will not certainly die!* God has said they will die, now the snake says they will not, and so there is a contest of which voice to believe. It sounds like the snake's strategy is to undermine confidence in the divine word: *you* can make your own decisions about *good and evil* apart from God, so the snake insinuates, and there are independent alternatives that ought to be considered. In the mind of the hearer, the snake's assertions convey the impression that God is withholding some privileges or experiences, but these are available for the taking.

Such a rhetorical approach is effective because in v. 6 she begins to rationalize and conduct an inner debate that detours God's word, concluding that, after all, the fruit looks like it would be helpful for gaining wisdom. A sudden surprise is the presence of the man who evidently has been there the entire time, but failed to intervene. He partakes of the fruit along with her, and thus both are complicit. After they eat, do they realize the poison of the snake's words? If they didn't feel any shame before, things have now changed, and hence the makeshift clothing that somehow seems to be a futile attempt to cover up their guilt.

During this fateful conversation the Lord God has been walking around in the cool of the day, a relaxed disposition that will not be seen again for quite some time. When God calls out to the hiding man, the question (*Where are you?*) seems less a request for information and more of an opportunity to restore what has been broken. The man's blaming the woman—and by extension, blaming God for creating her in the first place—is hardly taking responsibility, but at least the woman admits she was deceived by the snake.

More questions than answers are prompted by this text, but God does respond with lengthy speeches to each of the participants, with consequences outlined. For the man, his toil will be hard and the ground uncooperative, while the woman will suffer the pains of childbirth (and raising the kids will be no less painful). First to be addressed is the snake, who is cursed and doomed to crawl on his belly while constantly feuding with humanity. A program of deception will continue, but there is also a cryptic notice in v. 15 that at some point an offspring of the woman will arise and strike the snake's head. The snake does not make another formal appearance in the story, although in all likelihood this cunning creature might be lurking somewhere in the background.

With the mention of pains in childbirth, Adam names Eve with an echo of the word for *life*, anticipating her motherhood to come in the next chapter. As for the temporary fig leaves, they are replaced as God clothes them with more durable *tunics*, and in many cases these the kind of garments worn by priestly or royal figures. Does this suggest that God still views humanity as possessing a regal status and that priestly dignity cannot be erased by any strategy of the snake? Regardless, they will need these clothes because they are about to embark on a very long journey. The last moments of the chapter return to the tree of life, now guarded by *cherubim*, supernatural sentries armed with swords of flashing fire. Human beings have been exiled from the garden, much like later Israelites will be exiled from their inheritance after the destruction of Jerusalem temple (with its Eden-like imagery).

At an unspecified point after these events, Eve gives birth at the start of Genesis 4, somewhere outside the garden. Her naming speech captures her mood in the moment—Cain's name means *possession*—but the name of his brother Abel means "fleeting" or "vanity." There are lots of sibling rivalry accounts in the story ahead, with jealousy often at the forefront. The grown brothers present offerings of thanks to God that reflect their work: Cain brings *some* of the fruits of the soil, whereas Abel presents the choicest portions of the firstborn of his flocks. Because God looks with favor on Abel's high-quality offering, there seems to be a difference in the attitude or internal posture of the two brothers.

Cain's angry response prompts a penetrating sequence of divine questions and warnings in v. 6, and the term *sin* occurs for the first time in the narrative. With a root meaning of *missing the mark*, sin is compared to a dangerous predator setting a trap, ready to consume an unwary victim. Akin to his parents, Cain does not heed God's word. In the previous chapter there is deception by the snake, now there is deception by a brother when Abel is murdered (albeit without the snake's subtle gaslighting). Even though he lies to both Abel and God, the killer is not treated as his crimes deserve. The *mark of Cain* is not specified, but it is clear that he too receives the sentence of exile and dwells in *Nod*, an unknown land that means "aimless wandering."

Genesis 4 concludes with a listing of Cain's descendants (vv. 17–26), although the identity of his wife is a tantalizing omission. When Cain builds a city and names it after his son, it appears to be a gesture of empire building and a rebellion against his sentence of restless wandering. His descendants are known for prolific technology (forging tools and musical instruments), and there is also a fragmentary anecdote that records the vengeance of Lamech, continuing the legacy of violence bequeathed by Cain. The last lines of the chapter circle back to another child of Eve, although this time her naming speech is more somber, and poetically eulogizes her lost son. At this time, the reader is also told, people *began to call on the name of the Lord*, but it is not specified whether this is an impulse of conscience or a cry of desperation.

Hour 3: Genesis 5–11

LISTS OF NAMES MAY not be easy to read, but they do serve to advance the timeframe and occasionally provide details that may be important for the forthcoming plot. In the case of Genesis 5, the extraordinarily long lives are jarring for the reader, but longevity won't last forever as we will see momentarily. Methuselah might hold the record at 969 years, but his father Enoch went a step further: *Enoch walked with God, and was not, for God took him* (v. 22). The most attention is focused on Methuselah's grandson Noah ("comfort") who receives a lengthy introduction and a naming speech. Noah resurfaces shortly in the story, but first there is a bizarre episode at the beginning of chapter 6 that stretches divine patience to the breaking point:

> *The sons of God saw the daughters of men, that they were good, and they took wives for themselves, from whomever they chose.* (Genesis 6:2)

Elsewhere the sons of God are divine beings or members of the divine council (e.g., Job 1–2), and here they produce the Nephilim, characters of legendary size and strength. God's initial reaction is to impose a kind of salary cap, that is, a restriction of the human lifespan to 120 years (with only a handful of individuals in Genesis who are exempt). God further observes the mounting wickedness of humanity, whose every thought is consistently bent on evil. Cain was earlier warned that sin is like a beast setting a trap outside the doorway, and it would appear as though sin is certainly rampant in every sector of the earth. Such a condition prompts both divine sorrow (God is *grieved in the heart*) and a drastic decision. This could be the end, but now we realize the significance of Noah, who *finds favor in the eyes of the Lord.*

When Noah is warned of the coming floodwaters of judgment because of lawlessness on the earth, we discover that he and his family will be able to survive by constructing an *ark* (the Hebrew word is *tevah*). Some interpreters might describe a watercraft, but the ark can also be imagined as a sanctuary built for buoyancy on the waters of chaos; indeed, the later Jerusalem temple has some features in common with the ark. Here in Genesis 7–8 the ark preserves a remnant of humanity and animals during the forty days of rain that reverses creation and returns the earth to primeval chaos, as even the highest mountaintops are covered with swelling waters. But a key transition occurs at the outset of chapter 8:

> *And God remembered Noah, and all the beasts and all the cattle that were with him in the ark, and God caused a wind to pass over the earth, and the waters receded.* (Genesis 8:1)

On numerous occasions in the story God will *remember*, but it does not mean that something was forgotten. Instead, it is the activation of a previous commitment, and here the covenant with Noah is the basis for divine action. The term *covenant* is used in chapter 6 and repeated in chapter 9 (think of a binding pact between a powerful master and subservient underlings, with commitments and responsibilities for both parties), and various covenants are enacted before the Bible is finished. A sequence follows in the wake of God's remembering: the floodwaters subside and a dove returns to the ark with a olive leaf, along with the sign of the rainbow and a divine soliloquy pledging to never again doom the earth despite the evil machinations of the human heart.

After disembarking, however, scandals start to unfold. Despite a renewed invitation to be fruitful and fill the earth, Noah's drunkenness in Genesis 9 sets off a chain reaction that results in the cursing of his grandson. Although Canaan is a character here, the *land of Canaan* will be transferred to another family as Genesis continues. Noah may have been considered "righteous in his generation," but the flood does not cleanse his own impurities nor those of his descendants. Noah's sons branch out to various parts of the earth, as the table of seventy nations in chapter 10 tacitly introduces many of the nations and kingdoms that populate the forthcoming narrative. But the opening of chapter 11—flashing back to a time when the world still has a single language—narrows the geographical focus to a particular region and its ambitious architects:

> *They said, "Come, let's build ourselves a city with a tower, with its top in the heavens! Then we'll make a name for ourselves, lest we be scattered over the face of the whole earth."* (Genesis 11:4)

Due to their fear of being dispersed, these builders erect a skyscraper, and the Lord comes down to see it (so perhaps it's not quite as high as they would like to think, nor does it seem to get finished). They do gain a name for themselves, but the name is *babel*, from the root term "chaos/confusion." The reader should keep in mind that this is the founding narrative of the city of Babylon, which will be an infamous place and the source of disaster for God's people in the days ahead. In the aftermath of Noah's debacle and the tower enterprise, it might be thought that God should give up on humanity. But at the end of chapter 11 there are some new figures introduced, specifically Abram and Sarai. Although the genealogy in 11:27–32 seems innocuous enough, the world is on the threshold of an entirely new plotline and promise.

Hour 4: Genesis 12–24

THE BOOK OF GENESIS can be divided into two main parts, chapters 1–11 and 12–50, and both parts begin with a decisive word of God. In the first part, God speaks and transforms the earth from chaos into life; in part two, God's word creates new hope for the world by means of a promise to an individual family. That this family will be the vehicle of hope is first glimpsed in the migration recounted at the end of chapter 11. The tower builders want a name for themselves, but all they get is *babel* (confusion), whereas by contrast God promises to make Abram's name great. At the outset of chapter 12 the defining word is quoted, as God directs Abram to journey from Ur of the Chaldeans (Babylonian territory) to a new land: here God will make him into a great nation, and through him all the families of the earth will be blessed.

By any measure this is an astonishing promise, but any fulfillment looks unlikely as it is revealed that Abram is seventy-five years old, has no children, and Sarai his wife is barren. On the one hand, into the dark abyss of Genesis 1 God's word brought forth light and life, so it is certainly possible in chapter 12 as well. On the other hand, decades will elapse before there are any signs of fulfillment, and no doubt the characters will be frustrated. So Abram deserves some credit for making the trip to Canaan and traversing the land, all without any recorded speech. But matters soon take an ambiguous turn when a famine occurs in the land. Egypt, with the Nile River and bountiful annual harvests, is a perennial temptation for later Israelites. Abram opts for Egypt, and his first direct speech is addressed to his wife Sarai just as they are crossing the border:

> *"Behold, please, I know what a beautiful woman you are, and when the Egyptians see you, they will say: 'This is his wife!' They will kill me, but let you live. Please say that you are my sister, in order that*

> *it might go well for me, and so my soul can live because of you."* (Genesis 12:11–12)

Sarai is duly taken into Pharaoh's house and Abram reaps material benefits, but God inflicts serious diseases upon Pharaoh. Presumably these drastic measures are to protect the promise that has been jeopardized by this trip to Egypt, and periodically God will have to intervene in similar predicaments. Abram emerges from chapter 12 as someone capable of impressive faith, but also with frailties. If the reader is expecting lofty tales of spiritual heroism, a quick glance at the rest of his career from chapter 13 onward does not quite provide that. Instead, there is a mixed bag: some high moments but also many tensions and ambiguities, and it takes decades before any aspect of God's promise appears to be fulfilled.

Military prowess is on display during Abram's rescue of his nephew Lot in Genesis 14; in the previous chapter they have to separate on account of their vast possessions, but Abram shows courage after Lot is taken by a coalition of Canaanite kings. There is a reiteration of the divine promise and a covenant ceremony in chapter 15, but it is followed by a flawed attempt to secure an heir through surrogate motherhood in Genesis 16, resulting in the birth of Ishmael. In chapter 17 the names of our key characters are changed to Abraham and Sarah, and we should note that whenever there is a change of name from this point onward in the story, it usually marks a change in destiny. The seal of circumcision is also announced, and God provides assurance that Sarah herself will give birth to a son despite her advanced age of ninety years. Once more Abraham tries to pass Sarah off in Genesis 20 (*sister act II*), but nonetheless Isaac ("laughter") is born in chapter 21 exactly as God forecasts. Domestic strains can be felt when Ishmael is banished, but even more arresting is the climactic episode in chapter 22:

> *After these things, God tested Abraham . . . "Take your son, your only son whom you love, Isaac, and go to land of Moriah: there, you will offer him as a burnt offering on one of the mountains I will tell you."* (Genesis 22:1–2)

Human sacrifice may have been a grim reality in Canaan, but it is roundly condemned in the Bible. Hence the reader is told at the outset this is a *test* for Abraham, using the same verbal phrase *go* (*lekh-lekah*) as in chapter 12 when he sets out from his homeland. Carrying the wood, Isaac's nervous question about the missing lamb for the sacrifice is soon offset by his father's binding; indeed, this haunting episode is often referred to as the *akedah* (from the Hebrew verb *to bind*). The unbearable intensity of Isaac bound on the altar is finally broken as God intervenes at the last second with a commendation (*Now I know that you fear God*) and another reiteration that Abraham's descendants will be as numerous as the stars of heaven.

Moriah, incidentally, is only mentioned again centuries later in 2 Chronicles 3:1, in connection with another place of sacrifice, the Jerusalem temple. As for Abraham, having passed this excruciating test he later purchases a burial cave upon the death of Sarah. This cave is his first legal possession in the land. The plot continues in Genesis 24 when Abraham secures a bride for Isaac, Rebekah, and thus the story proceeds even though the larger promises have yet to be fulfilled. Eventually Abraham is buried in the same cave as his wife (25:9). Ironically, it will be a crowded grave before long, as other descendants of the once childless Abraham are likewise laid to rest there as the story continues (e.g., Isaac, Rebekah, Jacob, and Leah; see Genesis 49:29–31).

Hour 5: Genesis 25–36

REBEKAH IS BARREN LIKE Sarah before her, and so a pattern is starting to emerge. At the midpoint of Genesis 25 Isaac prays for his wife, and she conceives, but she also receives a divine oracle about the twins in her womb: in a reversal of the usual firstborn status, *the older will serve the younger*. These *two nations* fighting in the womb prefigures their later struggles, even as their names ("hairy" and "heels") capture the personalities of these two characters. Esau/Hairy is the firstborn, yet Jacob/Heels stews up a plot to take the birthright (that is, the double portion of the inheritance; see Deuteronomy 21:17). While Esau is guilty of despising the birthright, Jacob's conduct raises questions about his moral compass, to say the least, and such problematic aspects are poised to increase.

Isaac is the quietest of the major characters, but has a starring role in a couple of important episodes: in Genesis 26 he too falls back into the habit of the *sister act*, and in chapter 27 he is blind and prepared to bless his firstborn Esau before his death. The blindness of Isaac is the basis of the elaborate deception by Jacob. Taking his cue from Rebekah his mother, Jacob masquerades as Esau (using his clothes and young goat skins) in order to deceive his father for the blessing, just as he steered his brother into giving him the birthright.

Despite Isaac's suspicions and perhaps because Jacob insists "I am Esau" while wearing his brother's clothes, Isaac pronounces an elaborate blessing in vv. 28–29. Discovering that he has been bamboozled, Esau asserts that his brother has "heeled" him and harbors a murderous rage, prompting Rebekah to send him to his uncle Laban in Haran. Laban is first introduced in chapter 24 when he is excited about the huge nose ring given to Rebekah, and he soon proves to be a worthy adversary for his nephew.

On the way to Laban's house, Jacob has a dream of a *stairway* in chapter 28, and unlike the Babel tower, its top actually does reach the heavens.

Even though Jacob obtains the blessing through deception, God reiterates that the promise to Abraham will continue through him, and he will return at some point to this same land his descendants will inherit. Upon awakening, Jacob names the place Bethel ("house of God"), a prominent Israelite city later on.

Another narrative pattern seen in chapter 29 is the romantic encounter at the well. Similar to Isaac back in chapter 24, Jacob meets his future bride, Rachel, at a well of water, although their relationship will be complicated. Arriving at his uncle's, Jacob is greeted with Laban's kiss, but we might recall that Jacob kissed his father even while he was lying to him (27:27). In the second half of Genesis 29 a wedding is organized for Rachel, so Jacob thinks. But Laban switches the brides at night and fools his new son-in-law. In the morning, Jacob is outraged when he finds the older sister Leah beside him, and confronts Laban:

> *"What's this you've done to me? I served you for Rachel, didn't I? Why have you deceived me?!"* (Genesis 29:5)

Laban explains the custom that the younger should not be preferred over the older, and then lays out a plan whereby Jacob can also marry Rachel in return for another seven years of labor. It would be hard to resist sensing a measure-for-measure scheme at work, as the deceiver is deceived and then complains about it (cf. 27:35–37). But there is no elaboration in the narrative, and so the reader is left to wonder if a hidden hand is at work. Nonetheless, from these two quarreling sisters (and their maidservants), twelve sons are born to Jacob, morphing into the twelve tribes in the later storyline. For her part, Rachel is barren, no doubt contributing to the stresses and rivalries of the household, but miraculously gives birth to Joseph in chapter 30.

During his lengthy stay Jacob accumulates lots of livestock, mostly at Laban's expense. Combined with a divine word and an increasingly tense relationship, Jacob decides to return to Canaan. Perhaps Jacob slinks away, but after catching up with the caravan and a long exchange in chapter 31, Laban seems content to part on reasonable terms (albeit without any goodbye kiss to his son-in-law). But a momentous event takes place near the end of the journey in Genesis 32, as Jacob ventures to the riverbank at night. There he begins to wrestle with a mysterious assailant who refuses to disclose his name, but does confer on Jacob the name *Israel* (which might mean "God prevails"). Jacob names the places *Peniel* ("face of God") and walks away from the encounter with a permanent limp.

Prior to the wrestling match, Jacob had sent a lavish gift ahead to his brother Esau, who had earlier been stewing in a murderous rage because of the stolen blessing. Jacob is understandably frightened when he hears a report of Esau marching toward him with 400 companions. In Genesis 33 Esau runs toward his brother, grabs him, and welcomes Jacob home in what is surely among the most unexpected reunions in literary history. Nonetheless, life back in Canaan is not without trouble. In chapter 34 there is violence and deceit by two of his older sons, revolving around their sister Dinah. Moreover, Rachel dies in childbirth when Benjamin is born, and the firstborn Reuben sleeps with his father's concubine, pointing to household fractures. Yet in Genesis 35:9–12 God appears to Jacob and reiterates both his change of name and the promise, noting that kings will come from his line. So, the reader acknowledges the dubious side of Jacob's character, but also the strength of God's commitment, and wonders if this might echo the life of the nation of Israel as the story continues.

Hour 6: Genesis 37–50

Focus turns to the sons of Jacob in the concluding section of Genesis, an extended and powerful narrative with interlacing plotlines. If Jacob had some dubious moments, his sons certainly follow in his footsteps. The central character is Joseph, introduced as his father's favorite in chapter 37, and given a special robe as a sign of his status. Not only does he bring Jacob a bad report about his brothers, but he also has dreams of supremacy that inflames their anger. It is Judah's idea to sell Joseph as a slave for some silver, and they deceive their father with a young goat in an ironic echo of Jacob's own fatherly deception back in Genesis 27.

Meanwhile, Joseph is purchased as a slave by one of Pharaoh's officials, but in chapter 38 Judah moves away from the family tents. His coarse treatment of his daughter-in-law Tamar paints him in negative light, but when Judah unwittingly impregnates her, she triumphs in the end: Judah is forced to concede *she is more righteous than me*, and from Tamar the line of David will eventually arise. In a pointed contrast, Joseph resists the seduction of his master's wife in Genesis 39 after he is promoted, but despite his virtuous words (*how could I do this wicked thing and sin against God?*) her false accusations get him thrown in jail.

Repeatedly we are told that God is with Joseph, but it is still hard to fathom a more depressing scenario: he was sold as a slave by his own brothers, and is now imprisoned on trumped-up charges. Perhaps he is a bit spoiled earlier in the story, but his response to adversity is impressive. But something unexpected happens: because of the incarceration, he interprets the dreams of other jailed servants of Pharaoh, paving the way for his ultimate promotion in chapter 41, when he interprets the royal dreams and predicts seven years of famine. Joseph succeeds where the magicians fail, and is rewarded with a high-ranking position, new clothes, and a family. The names of his sons Manasseh (*God has made me "forget" all my trouble and all my father's household*) and Ephraim (*God has made me "doubly fruitful" in the land of my affliction*) provide an internal perspective on his ordeal (41:51).

As the second-in-command Joseph orders the construction of storage facilities to prepare for the famine, and when it duly arrives, caravans start traveling to Egypt to purchase grain under his supervision. Famine takes Abraham to Egypt earlier in chapter 12, and now in chapter 42 Joseph's brothers likewise make the trip. A dramatic moment soon occurs when they are face-to-face with the governor of Egypt: the brothers don't recognize Joseph, but he recognizes them, and through an interpreter procures information about his father Jacob and young Benjamin, who is still in Canaan. Joseph seems to be testing them when he imprisons Simeon and demands that Benjamin be brought down before him. As Joseph treats them harshly, the brothers start to experience guilt for their earlier conduct, and they debate with one another:

> *"Truly we're being punished because of our brother, for we saw his soul in distress when he begged us for mercy, and we didn't listen. That's why this distress has come upon us!"* (Genesis 42:21)

On the way back home, one of the brothers discovers the silver has been returned to his saddlebag, and their trembling intensifies: *what is this that God has done to us?* (42:28). They earlier sell Joseph for silver, and now silver is used to start exposing their guilt. If their father Jacob had some lingering suspicions about Joseph's fate many years earlier, he further senses that something is amiss when he sees the silver (does he suspect that they sold Simeon as a slave?). He refuses to allow Benjamin to accompany them back to Egypt, and this reluctance imperils the family as the famine worsens.

Judah steps up in chapter 43 with a guarantee for Benjamin's safety that allows the brothers to return to Egypt and have another audience with the governor who has taken a peculiar interest in them. No doubt their anxiety increases when an officer brings them into the house for a banquet and seats them in exact birth order. They are dismissed at the start of chapter 44, but the "stolen" silver cup planted in Benjamin's suitcase sets the stage for one more twist. When the evidence is found, the brothers do not sell out Benjamin as they once sold Joseph into slavery. Moreover, when the Egyptian commander insists that Benjamin alone is to stay behind as a slave and the rest can go free, Judah moves forward with the longest speech in Genesis and a daring proposal:

> *"Please let me remain as a slave instead of the boy . . . I beg you not to let me see the misery that would consume my father!"* (Genesis 44:33–34)

Previously Judah hatched the plan to sell Joseph as a slave, yet now he volunteers to become a slave so Benjamin can return to his father. This offer of substitution causes the "Egyptian" governor to exclaim *I am Joseph*, to the stunned silence of his brothers. It also sets off a series of events that result in Jacob and the family relocating to Egypt in chapter 46, in order to survive the famine. Several notable things take place in the closing chapters, including Jacob's audience with Pharaoh and his final words directed to his sons and their descendants. But after Jacob's death in chapter 50, the brothers are afraid that Joseph will seek revenge with their father out of the picture. They send a fake message to Joseph and bow down before him, but he responds with remarkable wisdom:

> *"Don't be afraid, am I in the place of God? You designed evil against me, but God redesigned it for good in order to bring about what is now happening: the saving of many lives."* (Genesis 50:19–20)

Not only does this speech capture the theme of the Joseph narrative, but it also reveals a key theme in Genesis as a whole: God consistently turns the nasty deeds of the human characters into something with a more beneficial outcome. It might be expected that this theme will continue going forward. Joseph's final words hint that God will *come to the aid* of the Israelites in Egypt, casting an ominous cloud over the next installment of their history. With the closing image of *a coffin in Egypt*, the Genesis story calls out for a sequel.

Hour 7: Exodus 1–10

The seventy descendants of Abraham at the beginning of Exodus indicate that God's promise is still moving toward fulfillment. But Abraham was also told that his offspring *would suffer in a land not their own for 400 years* (Gen 15:13). At first, life is abundant, and after decades of barrenness in Canaan there is vast fertility in Egypt. Such numerical growth, however, has the unintended consequence of catching the attention of a malevolent new king, who initiates a program of subjugation and slavery despite Joseph's earlier contribution. Even worse for the Israelites, the new king orders that infant boys be killed at birth, and when that policy fails—because of the clever and courageous help of midwives—he orders that they be drowned in the Nile River.

Resistance that begins with the midwives in chapter 1 continues with a mother in chapter 2. She is from the tribe of Levi—soon to be the priestly tribe for the nation—and she places her child in a *tevah*. Often translated as papyrus "basket," it is actually the same term as Noah's "ark" (*tevah*), the only other occasion the word is used in the Bible. Just as Noah's ark is essential for the survival of humanity, so this smaller ark carries hope for another rescue. Drawn out of the chaotic Nile by none other than Pharaoh's daughter, the youngster is ironically adopted into the Egyptian royal household. She gives him the name *Moses*, playing on the idea of "bringing through the water," and foreshadowing the aquatic experience to come for the beleaguered Israelite slaves.

Moses looms large in the next four books, but his career has a controversial start as he murders an Egyptian and then deals with barbed questions from a fellow Israelite ("*Who made you a prince and a judge over us?*," anticipating leadership struggles to come). Pharaoh hears about the matter (2:15), but is he angry because of the murder, or because he only now realizes that he has unwittingly harbored a Hebrew in his own house? Moses escapes by fleeing to Midian, and his eastern flight evokes memories of Jacob: a questionable deed prompts an escape, where he meets a wife by a well, and has a divine encounter. As Exodus 3 begins, the effects of Moses's experience will reverberate throughout the storyline:

> *Now Moses was leading the flock of his father-in-law, the priest of Midian. He drove the flock beyond the wilderness, and came to the mountain of God, to Horeb. And then, the LORD's messenger appeared to him in a flame of fire from the midst of the thornbush. He looked, but behold, the thornbush was burning with fire, yet the thornbush was not consumed.*

From the fire God announces—having heard the cry and felt the pain of the Israelites—that Moses is to confront Pharaoh and demand their release. Objecting strenuously to his commission during this long dialogue, Moses's protests are each met with a divine response and a series of *signs*, starting with a revelation of God's name. Although a bit cryptic, the name of the Lord uses a configuration of the verb "to be." This underscores that God *is*, *has been*, *will be*, and also that God is the one who *causes* things to happen. The meaning of this name will be demonstrated dramatically in the land of Egypt, when against all odds the Israelites are unchained and the mighty Pharaoh is humbled.

But before that, Moses's return to Egypt begins with a very strange moment in Exodus 4:24–26 when he is nearly destroyed, and a reunion with his older brother Aaron, who appears for the first time in the narrative. Together the reunited brothers are embraced by the Israelites and then, at the outset of chapter 5, confront Pharaoh. If they were expecting an immediate release, Pharaoh's loud refusal quickly dispels such notions, and instead the slaves' burdens increased as they now forced to make *bricks without straw*. Harsher conditions cause resentment among the Israelites (5:21–22), prompting Moses to complain to God, who does *not* seem to be making anything happen at all.

Earlier God had declared that signs and wonders would be multiplied in Egypt (4:21), and in chapter 7 the stage is set for a memorable display in the royal court. Aaron throws down his staff and it becomes a *tannin*, usually translated as a snake but more likely a dragon or a sea monster. The Egyptian magicians do the same thing with their secret arts, but the display ends when Aaron's staff ingests the others. The *tannin* is a preview of the sequence of ten plagues that follow, and it is probably not a coincidence when the Nile is turned to blood as a reminder of the genocide in chapter 1.

Once more, the magicians replicate the feat, but why not just turn the river back into freshwater? Frogs in the bedroom must have been particularly annoying, and after the lice and mosquitoes, frustration mounts in Egypt:

> *The magicians then said to Pharaoh, "This is the finger of God!" But Pharaoh's heart was hardened. He did not listen to them, just as the Lord had said.* (Exodus 8:19)

At various points God hardens Pharaoh's mind, but at other points Pharaoh stiffens his own resolve. Does God do some cognitive rewiring (as in the movie *Inception*), or is this a combination of stubbornness and a larger battle against the gods of Egypt (cf. 12:12), as Pharaoh wavers while Egypt is destroyed? The time frame of the plagues isn't specified, but it sounds like a steady parade: livestock, boils, thunder and hail, locusts. Elements of the created world are redeployed, that in the end will actually result in the new creation of a nation rescued from chaos. After eight plagues, the ecological disaster emphasizes the range of God's control, yet increasingly the Israelites are exempt from much of the calamity. Back in Genesis 1, darkness covered the face of the deep, and in a return to a primordial mess, the ninth plague features *darkness that could be touched* (10:21). Pharaoh may think it cannot get worse, but the climactic tenth plague is still to come.

Hour 8: Exodus 11–19

HAVING DECLINED MANY OPPORTUNITIES to release the Israelites, the tenth plague—anticipated earlier in 4:22–23—on the firstborn is announced to Pharaoh in chapter 11. The next phase of the story has a slightly different chronology, as instructions for future commemorations of the Passover are interwoven with real-time events in Egypt. The Israelites are carefully told to apply the blood of a lamb on the doorframes of their houses so that destruction will *pass over* them, and these lengthy instructions underscore the importance of always remembering this defining moment of escape from slavery. Notably, the plague itself is tersely narrated in 12:29–32, in keeping with its gravity, and the loud cry in v. 30 is a reminder of the Israelite cry because of their suffering (3:7, 9).

At the end of 430 years in Egypt (see 12:40), the descendants of Israel are driven out by the overpowered Pharaoh, sent off so quickly that their dough has no time to rise (and commemorated annually in the Passover and the Feast of Unleavened Bread). But in chapter 13 the people are not allowed to use the more direct coastal route lest they be scared by the threat of war. Instead, they are led to the Red Sea *by way of the wilderness* through an unprecedented GPS system: a pillar of cloud by day and pillar of fire by night. But the liberation is temporary, as Pharaoh and the chariots of Egypt start chasing after the slaves in chapter 14. Seemingly trapped with the Red Sea in front of them and the army right behind, the Israelites voice a complaint, *Were there no graves in Egypt that you've taken us to die in the desert?* However, the Israelites soon observe that *both* the chaotic waters and the pursuing army are about to be vanquished before their eyes:

> *Moses stretched forth his hand over the sea, and the Lord walked back the sea with a strong east wind all that night. He turned the sea into dry ground, and the waters were divided. And the Israelites went through the midst of the sea on dry ground, with the waters as a wall for them on their right and on their left.* (Exodus 14:21–22)

There is no indication that the Egyptians are impressed with the divided sea as they relentlessly pursue the Israelites, but God causes confusion in their ranks and the wheels quite literally fall off their chariots. Moses once more stretches out his hand, and when the waters of the sea come crashing back on Pharaoh and his army, an ironic reversal is apparent: earlier the Egyptians had tried to destroy the Israelites through drowning, only to now be drowned themselves. The exodus event is a watershed moment in the story, and the reverberations of this rescue are felt throughout the Hebrew Bible and into the New Testament as well.

The Israelites celebrate this victory through the "Song of the Sea" in chapter 15, a poetic composition with several movements that emphasize God's sovereignty over the chaotic waters, the utter subjugation of Pharaoh, and the assurance of divine guidance in the journey to Canaan and beyond. The reliability of God is applauded in these optimistic lyrics, but the wilderness is a dangerous place with harsh terrain and a lack of resources. Three days after the spectacular deliverance at the Red Sea, the faith of the Israelites is put to the test with a different kind of water crisis in 15:22–27, as they cannot drink the water at a place called *Marah* ("bitter"):

> *Then the people murmured against Moses, saying, "What are we to drink?" He cried out to the Lord, and the Lord directed him to a tree. He threw it into the water, and the water became sweet. There he made for them an inscribed rule, and there he tested them.* (15:24–25)

Such crises will be commonplace as the narrative continues, and chapter 16 immediately features a food shortage and another loud complaint as the Israelites long for the buffets of Egypt. Yet God meets their needs with *manna* (a Hebrew phrase that plays on "what is it?") and quail, along with various instructions to teach the community to follow directions. A serious military threat follows in chapter 17 with the Amalekites, desert-dwellers who launch an unprovoked attack. Without much military training, the Israelites prevail with divine help, and this episode provides a first glimpse of Joshua, who soon has a prominent role. On this journey to the mountain of God, the Israelites hear God describe them as a *treasured possession* uniquely set apart as *a kingdom of priests and a holy nation* (19:5–6). With Sinai wrapped in smoke, such words are a prelude to the defining encounter in the next installment of the story, unfolding the covenant relationship between God and this community.

Hour 9: Exodus 20–40

After the frantic pace and movement in the first half of Exodus, the second half of the book takes place at the single location of Mount Sinai: the same mountain where Moses experienced the fire of God's revelation back in chapter 3. This second part of Exodus also introduces the body of legal material that makes up a considerable percentage of the Pentateuch. Leading off in prime position is what is traditionally called the "Ten Commandments" at the beginning of Exodus 20, although a more precise phrase is *ten words* (see 34:28, and hence the term *Decalogue* is also used). It should be noted that divine grace is emphasized at the outset, and even the very first commandment is based on what God has already done:

> *And God spoke all of these words, saying: I am the Lord your God, who brought you out from the land of Egypt, from the house of slavery. You will not have any other gods before me.* (Exodus 20:1–2)

In the listing of the ten words there no penalties or punishments, and perhaps this is because the heart of the Torah might be understood as a response to divine grace and the various commands are a grateful obligation that recognize God's rescue. These laws also reflect aspects of the divine character: so, the Israelites are enjoined to be faithful, honest, have respect for human dignity, and not be trivial with language, with each quality reflecting an attribute of God. Included within this section of Exodus 20–24 is a collection of various laws that form *the book of the covenant* (24:7), laws ranging from personal property and social justice to sabbath observance and annual festivals. An overarching goal, one senses, is the formation of a covenant community with a unique vocation on the earth. After Moses climbs the mountain with Aaron and his sons, along with seventy elders, they have an exceptional encounter:

> *They saw the God of Israel, and beneath his feet was what looked like a sapphire-blue pavement, clear as the sky itself. But he did not stretch out his hand against the Israelite nobles: they gazed on God, and they ate and drank.* (Exodus 24:10–11)

When the Israelites departed from Egypt, they did not leave empty-handed (3:22; 11:2), but received valuables from their neighbors. Now in chapters 25–31 these items of gold and silver provide the material for building the *sanctuary* (or *tabernacle*, from the term "to dwell"). Over a period of forty days and nights on the top of the fiery Mount Sinai, Moses receives the blueprints for the place where God dwells with the Israelites. In a sequence of seven speeches in Exodus 25–31 (reflecting the seven days of creation), directions for building the sanctuary are given, with images of Eden that reinforce the idea of God living in their midst (see 25:8).

At the center is the *ark of the covenant* (a different term from Noah's *ark*), a chest containing the tablets of the ten words. The other furnishings are designed to illuminate aspects of God's nature: so, the *table of bread* points to God's ongoing provision, while the *lampstand* is a visual reminder of the light of God's guiding presence. It should be kept in mind that the tabernacle is portable, and wherever the people travel, God's dwelling-place can always be at the center of their lives. These directions in chapters 25–31 are given a short time after the release from Egyptian slavery, and the reader might expect that construction of the sanctuary will now commence. But at the same time that Moses is intimately receiving these instructions at the top of the mountain, trouble is brewing in the next section of the story that threatens to tear the relationship apart:

> *Now the people saw that Moses was delayed in coming down the mountain, and so they assembled themselves before Aaron and said to him: "Get up, make for us gods who will lead the way before us! As for this Moses fellow who brought us up from Egypt, who knows what's happened to him?"* (Exodus 32:1)

Several episodes involving rebellion and complaint have already been seen in Exodus—usually surrounding issues of fear, food shortage, or water crisis—but chapter 32 presents the biggest disruption so far. Aaron complies with this dubious request, and in response to the gold-carved young bull, the community exclaims *These are your gods, O Israel, who brought you up out of the land of Egypt* in v. 4, and soon celebrates a festival. Here the reader might suspect that the people need to be set free from mental slavery as well, as it certainly seems like the gods of Egypt retain a firm grip on their minds. The Lord burns with anger, but Moses pleads for mercy, and as this lengthy episode unfolds God accommodates his request. A plague is sent against the people and the deadly sword of the Levites is wielded (anticipating their later role as the temple security force), and various aspects should be kept in mind because this is not the last rival sanctuary in the story (e.g., 1 Kings 12). Meanwhile, the material in chapters 33–34 indicate that God magnanimously forgives the community, a sense of restoration that is reflected in the face of Moses:

> *It came to pass that as Moses was coming down from Mount Sinai (and the two tablets of the Testimony were in Moses's hand as he came down the mountain), Moses didn't know that the skin of his face sent out a glow because he had been speaking with [the Lord]* . . . (Exodus 34:29)

Despite the debacle with the golden bull, the last section of Exodus 35–40 patiently recounts the building of the sanctuary with ornate details, including priestly attire, a bronze basin built from mirrors, and fragrant incense as a reminder of the abiding companionship of the invisible God. Prominent in chapter 37 is the ark of the covenant, placed behind a curtain and guarded by carved cherubim in the most holy place. It has been a year since the events of the Red Sea (see 40:17), and the people have been set free from building for Pharaoh and are now building for the Lord, having moved from slavery in Egypt to service for God in the wilderness. The final moments of Exodus include the presence of God infusing the completed sanctuary, with the Israelites poised for the next stages of their journey.

Hour 10: Leviticus

It is easy to overlook the book of Leviticus even though it is at the center of the Torah. Massive details that include everything from ritual procedure to dietary laws pose a challenge for contemporary readers. But overlooking this book means that we will miss important principles such as the sacred elements of creation and the command to *love your neighbor as yourself* (19:18). Leviticus takes place at the Tent of Meeting, emphasizing the majesty but also the approachability of God. Although the traditional title implies that the Levites who officiate the sanctuary are the primary recipients, a much wider audience is envisioned, with a goal of wisdom and spiritual discernment for the entire community. Here are four major movements or ideas in the book.

First, chapter 1 begins with God's word to Moses: "*When any one of you offers an offering to the Lord, you will bring your offering of livestock from the herd or from the flock.*" An array of various kinds of sacrifices and occasions are outlined in Leviticus 1–7. Some of these offerings are voluntary, while others are mandatory. At the top of the list in chapter 1 is the *whole burnt offering*, probably the most lavish sacrifice, and presented as an act of gratitude or sorrow. Other categories include *grain*, the *peace offering* that is shared with others, the *guilt offering*, and portions of food given to the priestly families. Unlike some other deities in the ancient Near East, the God of Israel does not need to be fed by humanity. Rather, these sacrifices are designed to cultivate a life of gratitude, generosity, and repentance. Sacrifices are a way to give thanks, or to restore relationship with God when individuals or the community drift off course.

Second, the wholehearted worship of the people is to be regulated by the priests, who are the focus of Leviticus 8–10. The sanctuary and its officials (Aaron and his sons) are dedicated for service in chapter 8, and perhaps mention of the number *seven* in the ceremony reflects the seven days in Genesis 1, a reminder that the sanctuary is place where chaos is replaced by order. In chapter 9 the sanctuary is now operational, and divine fire consumes the offerings as a signal of acceptance (v. 24), prompting the people to fall on their faces. But the most haunting moment in Leviticus occurs at the beginning of chapter 10 with an unexpected disaster:

> *Then Aaron's sons, Nadab and Abihu, each took his firepan and put fire in it, placed incense in it, and presented strange fire before the Lord that he had not commanded them. Fire came out from the Lord and consumed them, and they died in the presence of the Lord.* (Leviticus 10:1)

Most readers can sense the tremor that runs through this chapter, although it is not exactly clear what the strange fire is, nor how their tunics are not consumed in the flames (v. 5). But there is a poetic justice at work: they bring unauthorized fire into the holy place, and in turn are consumed by fire (in contrast to the fire of approval at the end of chapter 9). Aaron is silent, but at the end of the chapter he is speaking as a grieving parent.

Third, after the deaths of the two priests, chapters 11–16 delineate the categories of *clean* and *unclean*, having to do with boundaries and safeguards to the community's identity. Numerous subjects are covered in these chapters: dietary restrictions (11), childbirth (12), skin diseases and mildew (13–14), as well as bodily discharges (15). Nowadays, elite athletes are very careful about what they consume and avoid. In a somewhat similar way, the Israelites are rigorous about staying away from defilement and pollution with a respect for all of creation. If we consider mildew, for example, it festers in the dark, spreads like a contagion, and carries disease as it works its way through the closet and outward. Hence, it becomes an image of sin that must be dealt with and eradicated from the believer's life.

The high point of this section is the *day of atonement* at the center of the book in chapter 16, here envisioned as a focal point on the nation's calendar, as Aaron (and his later successors) cautiously walks behind the curtain to the most holy place. Two goats are included in this ceremony. One is sacrificed while the other is released into the desert carrying the failures of the people. The ritual is to be repeated year after year:

> *This will be an everlasting statute for you: in the seventh month, on the tenth day, you will humble your souls and do no work . . . for on this day atonement will be made to cleanse you, from all your sins before the Lord you will be clean.* (Leviticus 16:29–30)

Fourth, chapters 17–26 unfold an extensive holiness catalogue (with chapter 27 about dedicating things to God), punctuated with the phrase *be holy for I am holy* (e.g., 19:2; 20:7). Bear in mind that *Torah* is derived from the root "to throw (accurately)," and in this larger context relates to a wealth of instruction: just a short time ago the Israelites were an oppressed group without hope in a foreign land, but now have the chance for distinctive commitment to the God who rescued them. The final section of Leviticus includes everything from human sexuality to celebration of the festivals such as Passover or the Feast of Booths, and features a stirring reminder about the purpose of the exodus: *I will walk in your midst and be your God, and you will be my people. I am the Lord your God who brought you out from the land of Egypt as slaves for them, and I broke the bars of your yoke so you could walk with heads held high* (26:12–13). At the end of Leviticus the people are still at Mount Sinai, but about to continue their eventful journey toward Canaan.

Hour 11: Numbers

Having carried out their instructions, the Israelites have now constructed the sanctuary that is to be in the center of their camp and move with them wherever they go. Now, the people are poised to depart from the mountain and take a journey through the wilderness that is narrated in the book of Numbers. This next phase of the story has no shortage of wild episodes: fiery snakes and a talking donkey, water from a rock and a Hogwarts-like soothsayer, the earth opening up its mouth to swallow a group of rebels, and Aaron's staff (that once turned into a dragon) blossoming and then producing almonds. In geographical terms, it should be a fairly short trip from the foot of Sinai to the edge of the promised land. But as we will see, instead of lasting a few weeks, this journey takes an entire generation.

In terms of structure, we might divide Numbers roughly into three parts: preparation to leave (chapters 1–10), events in the wilderness (10–21), and affairs in the territory of Moab (22–36), just east of the promised land. The first ten chapters feature some large numbers, such as 603,550, the total count of fighting men. Among other things, such a population indicates how the promise to Abraham continues moving toward fulfillment. In Genesis 12 Abraham has no children, but now there is a vast nation preparing to return to the very land that was promised to Abraham hundreds of years earlier.

Other significant moments of Numbers 1–10 include: a census of the tribes and the arrangement of the camp (1–2), counting the Levites and instructions for transporting the sanctuary (3–4), a test for determining marital unfaithfulness that threatens the purity of the camp (5), and chapter 6 ends with the famous priestly blessing, *May the Lord bless you and keep you, may the Lord make his face shine upon you and be gracious to you* (see 6:24–26). Offerings for maintaining the sanctuary are outlined in chapter 7, while chapters 8–9 are mostly concerned with dedicating the Levites and the Passover celebration. In Numbers 10:10 the pillar of cloud lifts, and the Israelites set out. There might be a sense of cautious optimism as they proceed, but Moses's earlier protest back in Exodus 4:1 (*"But they won't believe me, they won't listen to my voice! They will say, God did not appear to you!"*) should be kept in mind.

The elaborate preparation for departure in the first section of Numbers is a challenge to read. But after the extensive buildup over many chapters, there is a quick deflation in the next few sentences. Days after leaving Sinai, it seems, the complaints begin. Nostalgic longing for Egypt occurs in chapter 11, as the riffraff conveniently forget their slavery and instead dream of *free fish, watermelon, and garlic* they claim to have enjoyed before the exodus. After getting stuffed to the nostrils with quail, the place is named *Graves of Lust* in the aftermath of a plague (v. 34). Such complaints are not limited to the riffraff, as Miriam and Aaron also get involved in chapter 12 when they bring up the skin color of Moses's wife, only for Miriam to be struck with a skin discoloration. But even more disastrous is the spy mission of chapters 13–14. A delegation of leaders are sent to explore the land, and forty days later return with this verdict:

> *"We entered the land where you sent us, and indeed it flows with milk and honey: here is its fruit! However, the people who live in the land are strong. The cities are fortified and really large, and we even saw descendants of the Anakites there!"* (Numbers 13:27–28)

Mention of the Anakites—an ancient race of giants—strikes fear into the community that the rousing minority report of Caleb and Joshua cannot offset. A negative report circulates through the camp, resulting in divine punishment of forty years of wandering in the wilderness. The reader might wonder what the spies were supposed to explore: the land, or the landscape of their unbelief? In the days ahead there will be many giant obstacles, but the Israelites themselves might be their own biggest opponent. There are expressions of divine patience, however, and the lengthy instructions in chapter 15 about sacrifices *to be offered in the promised land* signals some hope for the next generation.

Several other events in this section of Numbers should be noted, starting with the rebellion of Korah—Moses's Levite cousin, and thus someone who already has a privileged position—and his followers along with its aftermath in chapters 16–19. At issue is entitlement, that is, who is qualified to approach God. Despite talk about democratic nature of holiness, it sounds like envy and ambition are lurking below the surface. Korah does not seem to have taken seriously the leprosy of Miriam, and he too feels the sting of poetic justice: he opened his mouth in defiance, and the earth opens its mouth and swallows him. Although Moses's leadership survives the Korah incident, in a flash of temper he strikes at the rock in chapter 20, evoking memories of striking the Egyptian in Exodus 2. As a penalty, he will not lead the Israelites into Canaan, and so, like Korah and Miriam, Moses will end up buried in the desert outside the promised land. The people drink water from the rock, but after more grumbling in chapter 21 fiery snakes are sent among them. In response, God instructs Moses to make an image of what was destroying them:

> *So Moses made a bronze serpent and set on the signal pole: whenever someone was bit by a serpent, if they gazed at the bronze serpent, they would live.* (Numbers 21:9)

The third and concluding section of Numbers takes place in the region of Moab, east of Canaan. Balak king of Moab hires Balaam, a legendary soothsayer, to curse Israel in chapters 22–24, but Balaam ends up blessing the very people whom he is hired to curse: *For there is no divination against Jacob, no sorcery against Israel* (23:23). Balaam's lofty claims are satirically undermined by his talking donkey, but according to 31:16 he also gives advice about how to lure the Israelites to their downfall. There is massive damage in chapter 25 because of such enticement, resulting in more casualties led by the sword of Aaron's grandson Phinehas. Another census in chapter 26 records those born in the wilderness, indicating that Numbers is an account of two generations. In the end, generation "Ex" are brought out of slavery but are buried in wilderness, almost an answer to their rhetorical question at the edge of the Red Sea about *no graves in Egypt* (Exodus 14:11).

A new generation is the focus in the remainder of Numbers, and based on the itinerary of chapter 33 there are roughly forty stopping points during the forty years of wandering. The land of Canaan is finally within range at the end, but the journey has taken much longer than it should have. Still, the book closes on a more hopeful note in chapter 36 with the five daughters of Zelophehad, mentioned earlier in chapter 27. Since their father died without a son, they make the bold claim for the inheritance of their *future* descendants, even though they are *outside* of the land that has not yet been conquered. The five daughters lay claim to the promises of God, and are a faithful foil to the murmuring bodies buried in the wilderness of Numbers.

Hour 12: Deuteronomy

BACK IN EXODUS 4 Moses commented on his lack of eloquence: God was sending him back to Egypt, but Moses claimed he was unfit for the job because he was *heavy of mouth* (4:10). Whether he was bluffing or not, it is an irony that the book of Deuteronomy is presented as the longest speech in the entire Bible. There is a diversity of material in the book, but at the surface level it comes across as the memoir of Moses, a sweeping overview of the story of Israel filtered through the perspective of this peerless leader. This final address is delivered on the plains of Moab, just across from the promised land. If there is an intensity in these words, we recall that Moses will not be entering Canaan, and thus his last discourse does not lack urgency. Moreover, his audience is outside of the land, and is urged to enter, retain, and flourish in midst of its inheritance—a summons that certainly will be relevant for later generations as well.

There are lots of ways that Deuteronomy can be approached, but several broad movements in the book should be emphasized: the introductory speech in chapters 1–4, the long central section in 5–28 that includes an expansion of the Decalogue, and the concluding challenge, song, and burial of Moses in 29–31. But just before Moses begins his historical review in 1–4, the reader is told in passing that it should only take *eleven days* to travel from Sinai to the edge of Canaan. The first speech of Moses illustrates why it takes forty years, and how the community might avoid similar catastrophes in the days ahead. He recounts episodes from their march, providing a different angle on the setback of the spy mission, but also some success in battle against superior foes like the legendary Og king of Bashan (whose bed measured nearly fourteen feet long!). There also are some personal reminiscences, as Moses shares his thwarted desire to set foot in the land:

> *The Lord was furious with me because of you, and would not listen to me. He said to me, "Enough, don't keep talking about this. Go up to the top of Pisgah, and lift up your eyes to the west, and north, south and east, and see it with your eyes, for you will not pass over this Jordan river."* (Deuteronomy 3:26–27)

The long discourse in the central section of the book has another listing of the Decalogue (5:6–18), and it could be suggested that an extended application and template for modeling the Ten Commandments follows, ranging from honoring God at the designated place of worship (12:2–13:18) and observing the Sabbath (14:22–16:17), all the way to avoiding adultery (22:9–23:18) and covetousness (25:5–26:15). A series of potential curses are unfurled in chapters 27–28, with poignant images that describe a reversal of the exodus and a scattering into exile should the community opt for covenant disobedience.

One of the more famous biblical passages is featured in the central section of Deuteronomy, the *Shema* (from the verb "to hear") in 6:4–5, *Hear O Israel, the Lord is our God, the Lord alone! So, love the Lord your God with all your heart, all your soul, and all your strength.* Furthermore, there are continual reminders that even God's testing had a purpose, as the people are subject to hunger but given the gift of manna to realize that humanity *does not live by bread alone* (8:3; cf. Matthew 4:4). On the threshold of Canaan, the community is compelled to internalize afresh that their journey has brought them to a radically different point of view: just as God was faithful to bring the Israelites out of the smelting-furnace of Egyptian slavery, so God did not abandon them even during their worst days. Despite manifest rebellions, God has patiently led them from start to finish:

> *He led you through the vast and terrifying wilderness, with flaming snake and scorpion, through thirsty ground without water. He was the one who brought forth water from the rock of flint.* (Deuteronomy 8:15)

The final section of the book includes the last words of Moses, and his swan song in chapter 32. These lyrics, with a densely imagined origin story (*In a desert land he found him, in a wasteland howling and empty. He surrounded him, cared for him, guarded him as the apple of his eye*, v. 10), provide both a capstone and a poetic counterpoint to the earlier exhortations. This song also creates a jarring segue to Moses's mysterious burial notice in chapter 34: after a panoramic view of the land he will not enter, Moses dies with his eyesight *undimmed and his vigor unabated*, buried in a location God-knows-where (v. 6). But the words of Moses linger, and the final section also includes the climactic challenge to the people of Israel:

> *Look, today I have laid out before you life and prosperity, death and evil. I command you today to love the Lord you God, to walk in his ways . . . that you might live and multiply, and that the Lord your God will bless you in the land . . . but if your heart turns away and you don't listen, and are drawn aside to bow down and serve other gods, then today I announce to you that you will surely perish . . . So choose life, in order that you and your offspring might live*! (Deuteronomy 30:15–19)

In terms of structure, the speeches and the burial of Moses are both a conclusion and a beginning. Moses and the old generation give way to a new generation, a new leader, and the daunting task of taking possession of the land of Canaan. Deuteronomy functions as the end of the Torah, and the start the next installment of the story: the books of Joshua to 2 Kings. Moses's encouragement to walk with God and choose life become the dominant question for the following phases of Israel's journey: will the people be faithful and prosper in the land, or will disobedience and the threat of exile gradually gather momentum in the storyline?

Hour 13: Joshua 1–9

HAVING BEEN RESCUED FROM Egyptian slavery but reduced to wandering in the wilderness for an entire generation, the Israelites are finally poised to take possession of the land. The next sequence unfurls the long narrative of Israel's occupation of Canaan, starting with the book of Joshua, named after the main character and the nation's new leader following the death of Moses. While we can assume that Joshua was born as a slave in the land of Egypt, Joshua is first introduced in Exodus 17 as the assistant of Moses in the battle against the Amalekites. Not only is Joshua the assistant of Moses, but he is also one of the twelve spies in Numbers 13, and so has already set foot in the land. Although his parents name him Hoshea (*victory*), Moses renames him Joshua (*the Lord is victory*; Numbers 13:16). No explanation is given, so the reader might guess that it is to reinforce the idea—inscribed in his changed name—that the Lord is the only real source of any forthcoming success. In Deuteronomy 34:9 Joshua is mentioned again, and now will lead the Israelites across the Jordan and into Canaan.

Given the fortified cities and entrenched Canaanite occupants, it might be expected that the opening moments of Joshua would feature military advice and strategies for the conquest. Instead, there is a lengthy divine speech encouraging the new leader to hold fast to the Book of the Law, reciting it day and night: *so that you might carefully do all that is written in it, and then your way will be prosperous, and then you will act wisely* (1:8). It is unclear why Joshua secretly dispatches two spies to gather intelligence on the city of Jericho in chapter 2, and equally murky why they enter the house of a prostitute. Whatever the spies were looking for, they find a remarkable character who hides them from the king and forecasts the Israelite triumph. Although the two unnamed spies are clothed with ambiguity, Rahab emerges from this episode as an outsider, who, like the midwives in Exodus 1, defies the king, and shares some inside information:

> *"I know that the Lord has given you the land, and dread about you has fallen on us and all the inhabitants of the land melt with fear because of you . . . for the Lord your God is God of heaven above and the earth beneath."* (Joshua 2:9–11)

The Jordan may not be one of the largest rivers of the ancient world, but it does represent a boundary, and in chapters 3–4 the Israelites cross this threshold. Led by the priests who carry the ark of the covenant, crossing on dry ground evokes memories of the exodus and suggests that just as God brought them out of Egypt, so God will be with them as they enter the land. Not only do the Israelites undergo ritual circumcision and celebrate the Passover once they cross, but the manna also ceases and they now eat the produce of the land. As for Joshua himself, he has a numinous experience at the end of chapter 5 that reminds the reader of Moses and the burning tree on Mount Sinai. Meeting a figure with a drawn sword in the vicinity of Jericho, the figure declares that he is neither for Israel nor for their adversaries:

> *Then Joshua fell with his face to the ground and bowed low, and he said, "What would my master say to his servant?" The commander of the Lord's army said to Joshua, "Remove the sandals from your feet, for the ground where you are standing is holy." And Joshua did so.* (Joshua 5:14–15)

With its legendary high walls and perennial water supply, the fortified oasis of Jericho must be an imposing site, and this is the first city that the inexperienced Israelites need to overcome. God orders Joshua to encircle the city led by seven priests bearing the ark, and when the trumpets blast on the seventh day, the towering walls implode (6:20). Jericho is captured and all its inhabitants are destroyed, except for Rahab and her family. The frequency of seven might imply that a new order is imposed on the chaos of Canaan, an idea that enhanced by the fact that all the plunder of city is dedicated to the treasury of the Lord. If such compliance continues, then the Israelite campaign should be rather straightforward. But matters soon become more problematic.

Controversy rocks the camp when the next stage of battle results in an Israelite setback. Compared to Jericho, the city of Ai ("the ruin") should have been routinely conquered, but the Israelites are beaten back in chapter 7. Through a lot-casting ceremony, it is revealed that Achan from the tribe of Judah has acted unfaithfully. After getting caught Achan makes his confession about his actions during the invasion. When he admits to taking something off limits during the Jericho battle, it sounds similar to events much earlier in the garden:

> *"Truly, I've sinned against the Lord God of Israel. Here's what I did: I saw among the plunder a fine Babylonian coat, and 200 shekels of silver, and a 50 shekel tongue of gold. I desired them, and I took them. Behold, they are buried in the land within my tent, with the silver underneath."* (Joshua 7:20–21)

Jericho's plunder should have been dedicated to the divine treasury, but Achan acts treacherously, and along with his family, he is stoned to death in the Valley of Achor ("trouble"). Glancing back at the previous defeat, the notion of corporate responsibility comes to the fore, and the whole Israelite community suffers because of Achan. But after Achan is buried, Ai is successfully conquered—with some deft tactics and the signal of a raised sword—and this time the Israelites are granted its plunder to keep for themselves (8:27). But Achan's deed lingers, and along with the ambivalent spies of chapter 2, one might wonder if the new generation is that much different from the previous one, buried in the wilderness. A covenant renewal ceremony (cf. Deuteronomy 27) is enacted on Mount Gerazim and Mount Ebal at the end of chapter 8, with a list of blessings and cursings as a reminder of the necessity of obedience.

An alliance of anxious kings muster their troops at the outset of chapter 9, but one Canaanite group opts for a different survival strategy. The local Gibeonites act with cunning, outfitting themselves in worn-out clothes and carrying crumbly bread. They claim to be from a faraway country, and ask for a nonaggression pact. Without any divine consultation, Joshua and the elders make a covenant with them only to shortly discover the deception. Forever consigning them to be hewers of wood for the altar, when Joshua asks for an explanation, they answer: "*Because it was certainly reported to your servants that the Lord your God commanded Moses his servant to give you all the land, and to destroy all the inhabitants of the land before you. And so we greatly feared for our souls because of you, and we've done this thing*" (9:24). It is later disclosed that Gibeon is a larger city with ample warriors (see 10:2). Listening to this response, the Gibeonites have more in common with the testimony of Rahab than the deception of Achan, and they survive by recognizing the divine hand that is guiding the Israelites.

Hour 14: Joshua 10–22

At the beginning of chapter 9 there is an alliance of kings gathering to face the Israelites, but the story is interrupted by the deception of the Gibeonites. That thread resumes in Joshua 10, with an eventful episode that might be described as "the battle of five armies." The decision of the Gibeonites to join with Israel arouses the hostility of the king of Jerusalem (a city that will soon become the spatial center of the rest of the biblical storyline). Joshua and the Israelites are called to help their unlikely new allies who are now under attack from their neighbors, initiating a fresh round of conflict. After they march all night, God supernaturally comes to their aid, sending *stones from heaven* and responding to Joshua's prayer for an extension of daylight to seal the victory against the Canaanite coalition:

> *And the sun stood still, and the moon was motionless, until the nation was avenged on its enemies. Isn't this written in the Book of Jashar? The sun remained in the middle of the sky, and did not hurry to set for an entire day.* (Joshua 10:13)

Ravaged by such meteorological phenomena, the five kings are forced to hide in a cave that soon becomes their tomb. After their execution, the rest of chapter 10 contains a rapid-fire list of southern cities that are destroyed. The campaign turns northward in Joshua 11 with similar effect (against Jabin king of Hazor, who leads a combined force *as numerous as grains of sand on seashore*), followed by a summary of conquests in chapter 12. It should be acknowledged that the barrage of violence in this section of Joshua has caused many modern readers to recoil. It is probably not a consolation to insist that such violence is limited to this particular historical moment, nor to mention that Israel (a nation of former slaves) will be similarly pillaged by more than one rapacious superpower down the road.

But it should also be pointed out that the story itself is not without internal tension. For example, many times the Israelites are warned not to intermarry with any of the Canaanites; but if they were all supposed to be wiped out, it does raise the question about how much annihilation actually happened. On balance, the conquest is not clear-cut, because some of the reported military advances in Joshua are seriously undermined in the next installment of the story, while other gains are quickly erased. Even the first battle of Jericho—which could have been a high point—was clouded with compromise, revealing divided loyalties that become further apparent later in the narrative.

Meanwhile, the next major section of Joshua 13–21 delineates the allotments of land granted to the various tribes, prefaced by the divine reminder that much of the land still needs to be taken (13:1). In these chapters, the southern tribe of Judah has the most extensive listing, while the house of Joseph (Ephraim and Manasseh) has the largest holdings of the northern tribes.

Caleb is given the city of Hebron in Judah, where he dislodges giants and cedes territory to his proactive daughter Achsah (15:16–17). Through lot-casting other tribes receive their inheritances, and cities of refuge (where, if you accidently kill someone, you can flee for safety) are designated on both sides of the Jordan. The Levites are distributed throughout the land and given towns and pasturelands within the various tribes.

An appendix in chapter 22 revisits the eastern zone of the Reubenites, Gadites, and the half-tribe of Manasseh. At the end of the book of Numbers, these groups were content to settle in the districts before the land of Canaan, and it was suspected that they were trying to evade the conflict. However, they do assist the other tribes (see Joshua 1:12–18), and duly return to their eastern settlements. But building an imposing altar nearly prompts a civil war, with allegations of Achan-like unfaithfulness. A delegation led by Phinehas is satisfied with their explanation, although their altar stands uneasily as a monument to lurking fears and fragile unity. In the days of Judges, a devastating civil war will not be averted.

Joshua's career winds down with two final speeches. The first, in chapter 23, begins with a personal retrospective, but also includes warnings about the snares posed by the nations that have not been dispossessed, and threats of impending exile if the community opts for disobedience. The second speech in chapter 24 takes place in the northern city of Shechem (see Genesis 35:4), in the context of another covenant renewal ceremony.

A historical review ranging from Abraham and the plagues of Egypt to Balaam in the wilderness and the city of Jericho is followed by a direct challenge about undivided loyalty:

> *"Now then, fear the Lord and serve him with sincerity and truth. Put aside those gods that your ancestors served beyond the river and in Egypt, and serve the Lord . . . choose for yourselves today who you will serve . . . but as for me and my house, we will serve the Lord."* (Joshua 24:14–15)

At the end of his life, Joshua is called *the servant of the Lord* like Moses before him (v. 29). The bones of Joseph, brought up from Egypt, are finally laid to rest, and the three burials in the final verses of the book raise the question of how the nation will fare now that the great leaders of the past are gone. While it is noted in 24:31 that the people serve the Lord during the generation of Joshua, the numerous mentions of temptations in the land and warnings of expulsion does create a sense of foreboding for the next pages of the story.

Hour 15: Judges 1–12

After the exhaustive lists of tribal allotments in Joshua, the scandalous collection of episodes in the book of Judges arrives with a jolt. The characters range from Eglon of Moab (an ancient Near Eastern Jabba the Hut) and Jael wife of Heber (with the nine-inch nail) to Abimelech (who suffers a broken skull) and Micah's mother (who seems to have an idolatrous shopping addiction). Nowadays the term *judge* probably evokes images of gavels and gowns, but in this book a *judge* is more of a warrior than a judicial figure. Altogether there are twelve judges—basically one from each tribe—and most of the land of Israel is covered in a south-to-north movement over the course of the book.

Chapters 1–2 resume the story from Joshua, and while there are some geographical advances, the conquest remains incomplete, and military failures occur because of a lack of spiritual resolve. A recurring fourfold pattern is apparent in Judges: the people rebel and abandon God, they are oppressed by a foreign adversary, they cry out to God for help, and God responds in a creative way by rescuing them through the hand of a judge so there is no doubt that they are saved through a divine intervention and not by their own strength. Over the careers of the various judges there is a gradual downward spiral into increasing darkness. By the time we reach Samson—the blinded last judge in chapter 16—the same Israelites who failed to capture territory early in the book are on the brink of devastating civil war.

Othniel of Judah and Ehud of Benjamin are the first judges, and perhaps the least problematic. The people act corruptly, and they are handed over to Cushan-Rishathaim king of Mesopotamia for eight years (3:7–8). This king has a menacing name (something like *the dark and doubly wicked one*), but when the Israelites cry out for help God raises up Othniel, who was earlier introduced when he marries Caleb's daughter Achsah: the spirit of the Lord comes upon Othniel, who defeats foes from the other side of the Euphrates. Although the land has rest for forty years, once more the people do evil in God's eyes, and are handed over to Eglon king of Moab. Crying out for help, the left-handed Ehud is raised up as a deliverer. Persuading the portly king to grant him a private audience, Ehud wields his concealed dagger, and the Israelites are soon rescued once more. There are six "minor" judges at several points in the book, often reflecting qualities of the major judges around them. Shamgar is the first of them, *who slew six hundred Philistines with an ox-goad* (3:31).

When the Israelites again do evil in chapter 4, they are sold into the hand of the Canaanite king Jabin, whose commander Sisera oversees 900 iron chariots. On this occasion, Deborah the prophet is judging Israel, and she commands Barak of Naphtali to lead the charge against Sisera. It is unclear why Barak hesitates, but Deborah exclaims that Sisera will be defeated and the glory in battle will go to another, *for the Lord will sell Sisera into a woman's hand* (4:9). When Jael wife of Heber lures Sisera into her tent and drives a tent-spike into his head, Barak (who has been in pursuit of the general when God throws the Canaanites into a panic) surprisingly discovers the fallen Sisera. Jael's triumph and Israel's victory is memorialized in the song of chapter 5, which poetically describes God's intervention in celestial terms: *From the heavens the stars fought, from their highways they fought against Sisera* (5:20).

Psychologists might ponder why the Israelites are consistently unfaithful to the God who brought them out of slavery. We again notice the same dreary cycle at the outset of chapter 6, as the people are attacked by hordes of neighboring Midianites pictured as *a vast swarm of locusts*. Threshing wheat in a winepress to hide it from these oppressors, Gideon of Manasseh is called to deliver Israel, but he is a character with some serious doubts (6:11–23). Back in Deuteronomy 12:3 Moses instructed the Israelites to "hack down" the idols of Canaan. The name Gideon means *the hacker*, and it is quite an irony that before he liberates Israel from the Midianites, he is first directed to hack down the *Baal altar* in his own father's house.

After bulldozing his father's Baal installation, in chapter 7 Gideon leads a drastically reduced contingent of 300 against the countless camels of Midian, and uses some torches and trumpets to orchestrate an enormous win: when they shout "*A sword for the Lord and for Gideon*," God turns the sword of each Midianite against his own comrade. Yet Gideon is a mirror of the nation in many ways, for after this triumph the second part of his career is clouded with conflict. Even though he inflicts considerable violence on his own people in chapter 8, he nonetheless is offered dynastic rulership owing to the victory over Midian:

> *Then the Israelites said to Gideon, "Rule over us—you, your son, and your son's son—for you have saved us from the hand of Midian!" Gideon said to them, "I won't rule over you, and my sons won't rule over you—the Lord will rule over you."* (Judges 8:22–23)

Gideon declines the offer, but also makes an ephod from plundered gold, and it seems to be an instrument for predicting the future. Moreover, Gideon states that God rules over Israel, but in chapter 9 his concubine gives birth to a son named Abimelech, whose name means *my father is king*. Abimelech seizes power in a gruesome way and is declared king in Shechem (a grim parody of the covenant renewal ceremony in Joshua 24). After a three-year reign of terror, Abimelech's crown is broken at the bottom of a tower—*Then a woman threw an upper millstone on Abimelech's head, and it crushed his skull* (9:53)—and he enjoys the dubious honor of being the first of many failed kings in Israel.

Any questions about a downward spiral are put to rest by Jephthah of Gilead, a figure rejected by his family but summoned to fight against the Ammonite because of his skill as a fighter in chapter 10. But Jephthah has other insecurities, and an ill-advised oath results in an unfathomable episode of child sacrifice. His unnamed daughter's speech ("*My father, you have opened your mouth to the Lord—do to me just as has come out of your mouth, after what the Lord has done for you: vengeance from your enemies, the Ammonites*") becomes an index of how far the nation has plummeted, and the subsequent slaughter at the fords of the Jordan in chapter 12 presages further catastrophes as Judges continues.

Hour 16: Judges 13–21

Having crossed the halfway point of the book, a miraculous birth in Judges 13 ought to provide a flicker of hope. Memories of Sarah, Rebekah, and Rachel giving birth to significant characters surrounds the unnamed wife of Manoah in Judges 13 with great expectations. An angel of God announces that her son will be a lifelong *nazirite* (from the verb "to devote"; cf. Numbers 6:1–21) and will begin to liberate Israel from the Philistines who have been controlling them for forty years. Based on Numbers 6, the various abstinences of the nazirite vow are usually temporary, but there is reason to hope that this next judge—the last in the book, as it turns out—will be a pillar of self-control in a culture of indulgence. His initial actions, however, create a different impression:

> *Samson went down to Timnah. He saw a woman in Timnah from the daughters of the Philistines. Then he went up and reported to his father and mother. He said, "I've seen a woman in Timnah, from the daughters of the Philistines. So now, get her for me as a wife!"* (Judges 14:1–2)

Intermarriage has been a vexing issue in Judges (see 3:6), but in this case Samson's attraction to a Philistine paradoxically becomes an occasion for God to commence a program of deliverance. There is an early display of uncommon strength as Samson tears apart a young lion, but also a recklessness one as he is rendered unclean when he eats honey from the dead body. The riddle contest at the wedding might be an opportunity to win a contest of wits, but Samson establishes his own mastery when stealing thirty sets of clothing (14:19) after his new wife reveals the answer to his riddle to the Philistines. He is clothed with the divine spirit despite manifestly self-centered behavior. In chapter 15 Samson is a figure of rage: upon discovering his wife is given to someone else, he catches 300 foxes that he ties tail-to-tail, and with his own version of Gideon's torch trick he strikes a blow to the heart of the Philistine economy. Even when handed over by his own people, Samson uses the unlikely weapon of a donkey's jawbone—although it too is unclean, since it is taken from a fresh corpse—but then demands water much like he earlier demanded that his parents secure for him a Philistine bride:

> *Extreme with thirst, he called to the Lord, and said, "You have given, through your servant's hand, this great salvation. And now, I'll die of thirst and fall into the hands of the foreskinned!" God broke open the hollow rock at Lehi, and water came out from it.* (Judges 15:18–19)

Samson survives a midnight liaison with a prostitute in Gaza, but events in chapter 16 prove to be his undoing. Several options can be suggested for Delilah's name, but certainly there is a resonance with the Hebrew term for *night*, and it is unclear if she is an Israelite. She has enough of a connection with the Philistines that the rulers offer her an exorbitant sum to sell out her boyfriend. Delilah's approach is not exactly subtle, but Samson must feel invincible as he toys with her obvious strategy. Increasingly, it appears that Samson is a picture of the nation: both have obligations (Israel to the Torah, Samson to his nazirite vow), both have been given expansive gifts from God, and both are categorically unfaithful. Samson's moment of reckoning comes after Delilah has his head shaved, and his descent into darkness is almost complete:

> *He awoke from his sleep, and said, "I will march out just like the other times, and I will shake loose." But he did not know that the Lord had turned aside from him. The Philistines seized him, and gouged out his eyes. They brought him down to Gaza, bound him with bronze chains, and he became a grinder in the prison. But the hair of his head began to grow after being shaved.* (Judges 16:20–21)

Humiliated as a spectacle in a Philistine temple, Samson does have one last prayer. Earlier he petulantly insists that God give him water, but his last prayer in 16:29 is humbler and more deferential. Not only is he strengthened one last time, but he destroys more of the oppressing Philistines *when he died than when he lived.* To what degree does Samson prefigure the later exile? Further down the road, the community itself will be taken as captives to a foreign land, and thus the cycle of judges ends with this caution.

A pair of concluding episodes revolve around the phrase *in those days there was no king in Israel*. Chapters 17–18 narrate the story of Micah, who apparently steals silver from his wealthy mother, but she then hires a craftsman to make yet another idol for the house of Micah. A wandering Levite is hired as a priest for this dubious but lucrative shrine, although in the end Micah himself is on the wrong end of a theft: a group of marauding Danites loot Micah's shrine, and the Levite sells him out. At the end of chapter 18 the name of the Levite is finally disclosed, and it is revealed that he is a direct descendant of Moses, an index of how far the nation has fallen.

The final scenes in chapters 19–21 are among the most appalling accounts in the entire Bible. This section begins with another unsavory Levite. After he retrieves his concubine, they lodge for the night in Gibeah of Benjamin. Unspeakable abuse takes place in this town, and it triggers an all-out assault against Benjamin, with the entire tribe nearly wiped off the map. The book of Judges begins with Israel taking territory, and now ends with the nation fighting against itself. Final images of maidens who are captured in order to repopulate Benjamin underscore the disintegration in the course of this book, capped with the concluding line: *In those days there was no king in Israel, and whatever was upright in someone's eyes, thus they would do* (21:25). Perhaps this sentence signals that with kingship, the people's fortunes will improve. Alternatively, it might indicate that things will grow even worse if the nation opts for a king to lead them.

Hour 17: 1 Samuel 1–15

Bracketing the book of Ruth for the time being—it will be covered in the Writings section of the Hebrew Bible—the book of 1 Samuel continues directly from Judges, and introduces *kingship* into the storyline. The opening chapters introduce Hannah and Eli and frame the issue of kingship from the perspective of these two characters. When barren Hannah gives birth to a son in chapter 1, it might be thought that Samuel will be the first king, but in fact he will be the first kingmaker in this complicated story of transition to a new political order. Hannah vowed to dedicate her son for divine service, and her song at the beginning of chapter 2 celebrates how God lifts the poor from humble circumstances, but also brings the arrogant crashing down: *The Lord will judge the ends of the earth, but will give strength to his king, and will elevate the horn of his anointed one* (2:10).

As she vowed, Hannah dedicates her young son Samuel to the sanctuary at Shiloh, visiting him every year and bringing him a royal robe. Eli the priest is responsible for the sanctuary, but there is rampant corruption. His sons Hophni and Phinehas steal from the offerings brought by the people, and Eli's own culpability is murky. At the end of chapter 2 a man of God unfurls a long speech of judgment against Eli's house (predicting the death of his two sons), and this looming judgment is reiterated in chapter 3 through God's words to young Samuel. Battle against the Philistines in chapter 4 proves disastrous for Israel, and an unnamed messenger from Benjamin frantically delivers the fateful news to Eli about the massive defeat:

> *"Also, your two sons Hophni and Phinehas are dead, and the ark of God has been captured." Then, just as he mentioned the ark of God, Eli fell off his throne backwards, beside the city gate. He broke his neck, and he died, for he was a very old man, and heavy. He had judged Israel for forty years.* (1 Samuel 4:17–18)

The captured ark is the main character in the next phase of the story, as this war trophy is taken into the temple of Dagon. But the god Dagon is soon dismembered (5:4) and the rest of the Philistines are struck with hemorrhoids. Such an uncomfortable predicament leads them to return the ark to Israel, through the mechanism of two milch cows who have never been hitched to a wagon. Yet the cows go straight down the road and end up in Beth-Shemesh, where 50,070 Israelites are struck down for looking into the ark (6:19).

Given the recent defeat at the hands of the Philistines, a victory where God thunders mightily in chapter 7 is an unexpected reversal. It can hardly be a coincidence that the chapter starts with a repentance ceremony, including the ritual of *pouring out water* that only occurs here, with a confession of sin and removing of other gods. But instead of any lasting change of heart, this episode is a temporary blip, and forms a jarring preface to the request for a king that will dominate the forthcoming storyline. The Gideon narrative has already illustrated the dangers of hereditary leadership, not to mention the frightening example of Abimelech's kingship in Judges 9, and more recently the sons of Eli. Chapter 8 starts with the report that Samuel appoints his sons as judges, but they pervert justice and accept bribes. It is not entirely clear if Samuel is aware of his sons' conduct, but their corruption seems to give the elders of the nation an excuse for their new demand:

> *Then all the elders of Israel assembled together, and came to Samuel, at Ramah. They said to him, "Look, you're old, and your sons don't walk in your ways. So now, appoint a king for us, to judge us, just like all the other nations."* (1 Samuel 8:4)

Samuel's angry reaction to the request for a king might be for theological reasons. In Exodus 19:1–6 God delivered the Israelites from slavery so that they can become a holy nation and a kingdom of priests. In other words, God is already their king, and the desire to imitate the surrounding nations amounts to a repudiation of that identity. But Samuel's anger might also be tinged with personal reasons as well; indeed, in verses 7–8 God reminds him *it is not you they are rejecting, but me they have rejected as king over them, just as they've done from the day I brought them out of Egypt*. God further instructs Samuel to warn them about the dangers of kingship, and Samuel then unfurls a long diatribe that describes everything the king will *take* from the people: they will regret their decision, Samuel says, and will cry out to God but get no response (8:11–18).

Despite the warning of royal exploitation, the people insist on a king who will lead them in battle. God consents to their demand, and in chapter 9 young Saul of Benjamin enters the fray. He is tall and handsome, but from the wrong side of the tribal tracks, recalling that Benjamin was nearly wiped out in the gruesome civil war at the end of Judges. Still, Saul's first impressions are favorable because (in contrast to the offspring of Eli and Samuel) he is an obedient son who goes in search of his father's lost donkeys. But things quickly go sideways for Saul once he is secretly anointed as king with a flask of oil, and then bombarded with a barrage of instructions, as Samuel tells him to go to Gilgal and *wait for seven days until I come to you, and I'll let you know what you should do* (10:8).

Saul may not perceive it, but this directive will prove costly to his leadership. Although Saul liberates the town of Jabesh-Gilead in chapter 11, the Philistines gather a fearsome force and prepare for battle against the panicking Israelites at the beginning of chapter 13. Saul waits for seven days, but Samuel has yet to arrive in Gilgal, and Saul offers the sacrifice. At that fateful moment, Samuel shows up and soon declares that Saul's kingship will not endure. Instead, *the Lord has sought out a man according to his own heart, and the Lord has appointed him as ruler over his people, since you haven't kept what the Lord commanded you* (13:14). The identity of this new leader is withheld for the moment, but it will not be Saul's son Jonathan (introduced in chapters 13–14). Jonathan is an impressive character, but will never have the chance to reign.

A second rejection of Saul's kingship occurs in the Amalekite debacle of chapter 15, and Saul does not emerge well from this battle against Israel's perennial desert foes. When Saul rips Samuel's robe when begging for forgiveness, Samuel reminds him that God has ripped the kingship from Saul and *given it to your neighbor, one better than you* (15:28). Toward this figure, the story now inclines in the second half of the book, and the complexities so far indicate that the issue of the monarchy will be a vexed one.

Hour 18: 1 Samuel 16–31

DESPITE SAMUEL'S OBJECTIONS, GOD orders him to Bethlehem of Judah to anoint a new king, and at a gathering of Jesse and his sons, God directs the prophet to anoint the one whom he indicates. When seeing the firstborn Eliab, Samuel concludes that he must be the chosen candidate, but God responds with a rebuke to look beyond the external: *for humans see the outward appearance, but the Lord sees right to the heart* (16:7). Having rejected all of Jesse's older sons, the youngest is finally brought from tending the sheep: he is a good-looking young man, and the divine spirit comes upon *David* after his anointing with the horn of oil. Meanwhile, Saul is being tormented by an evil spirit, but through curious circumstances David ends up in Saul's court as a music therapist. The situation gives rise to poignant irony, as the tortured incumbent can only be soothed by the one secretly appointed to replace him.

Like the Israelites, the Philistines are comparatively recent arrivals to the land of Canaan, and these two groups are vying for the same limited real estate. The Philistines, however, have the technological edge, and they also have a formidable giant who enters the stage in chapter 17. Goliath's armor is heavy and intimidating, and no Israelite agrees to fight him. For a second time David is introduced to the narrative, but his eagerness to engage in combat stands as a contrast to the rest of the army, and is only partially explained by the substantial rewards on offer. David's fighting words, both to Saul and then to Goliath whom he faces with only a staff and slingshot, reveal some uncommon courage:

> *"You're coming against me with sword, spear, and javelin—but I'm coming against you in the name of the Lord of Hosts, the God of the battle-ranks of Israel that you've taunted. Today the Lord will hand you over to me, and . . . this entire assembly will know that it is not*

by sword or spear that the Lord saves, for the battle belongs to the Lord, and he's giving all of you into my hand!" (1 Samuel 17:45–47)

In Judges 20 the slingshot is the Benjaminite weapon of choice, but here it is deftly deployed by David, and the giant crashes to the earth. The Israelite army pursues the fleeing Philistines, but David takes Goliath's head to Jerusalem: at this point the city is unconquered, although it is in the middle of the promised land, and anticipates Jerusalem's significance for the rest of the story. Not long after this unlikely victory, Jonathan gives David his robe and military equipment (18:1–4), perhaps as a kind of abdication, and foreshadowing the eventual reign of David in the days ahead.

Despite David's efforts against Goliath, there is no reward given, although he does eventually marry Saul's younger daughter Michal amidst rising popularity. Saul loved David when he first entered the court back in 16:21, but increasingly views him with suspicion, and even uses the marriage to Michal as an attempt to take him out. Hints of Saul's madness have already been seen, and appear to be confirmed as he throws a javelin at David's head on several occasions (18:11; 19:9). David escapes Saul's clutches through the timely intervention of Michal in 19:11–17, and this launches the long fugitive stage of the story, with David on the run from the manic Saul. During this period David gathers a band of fighters in the wilderness and seems to grow in strength (including taking another wife, the wealthy Abigail in chapter 26), and even finding refuge in Philistine territory. Saul's experience is the opposite in this phase, growing increasingly unhinged, such as when he massacres the priests at Nob in chapter 21. Yet Saul's life is spared on two occasions, and he is never successful in apprehending David.

The low point of Saul's career surely occurs in chapter 28 on a dark night in the northern village of En-dor. Against the inevitability of a Philistine offensive, in desperation Saul disguises himself to visit a necromancer, and of all people, has Samuel (whose death is recorded in 25:1) summoned for a conference. Why Saul would possibly want to visit with his antagonist is one of many mysteries in this episode, and the dead Samuel remains in an irascible mood: *Why have you agitated me by bringing me up?* (28:15). Saul explains his dire straits, but Samuel's news is grim, as he reminds Saul that God has ripped the kingdom from him and given it to David, and worse, *tomorrow you and your sons will be with me, and the Lord will give the entire camp of Israel into Philistine hands* (28:19). Witchcraft is prohibited in Israel (e.g., Deut 18:10–11), but the medium pleads for Saul—who falls to the ground upon hearing Samuel's prognostication—to rise and eat before departing. Saul heeds her words in the final moments of the chapter:

> *Now the woman had a fattened calf in the house. She hurried and slaughtered it, and took flour, kneaded it, and baked unleavened bread. She brought it before Saul and his servants, and they ate, and they arose, and they went away on that night.* (1 Samuel 28:24–25)

Saul goes to Mount Gilboa to face the Philistines in chapter 31, and enters a battle that he already knows will end with his death. First to be slain are his sons, including Jonathan, and as the noose tightens around Saul, he falls on his own sword. The Philistines impale his corpse on their temple wall, where it would have remained if not for the bold actions of Jabesh-Gilead. Prompted by memory of Saul's rescue in chapter 11 from Nahash the Ammonite, their valiant warriors take a risk to recover and bury the headless body of Israel's inaugural monarch, *and they fasted for seven days* (31:13). Saul's throne is now empty, but the fractious journey of kingship marches on.

Hour 19: 2 Samuel 1–11

Over the many years on the run from Saul, David steadily gathers allies and material wealth, and sends gifts to his southern supporters from his home tribe of Judah (1 Samuel 30:26–31). After Saul's demise, such generosity and alliances will prove strategic, and David often seems to be the smartest guy in the room. But before that, in the opening chapter of 2 Samuel, David gets the news of the defeat on Mount Gilboa, and orders his men to sing a funeral elegy: "*The splendor, O Israel, on your high places is slain, How the heroes have fallen!... Saul and Jonathan, beloved and beautiful! In life and death they were not parted, swifter than eagles, stronger than lions*" (1:19–27). David's poetic talent is on full display in these lyrics as he publicly mourns the loss of the king and his son Jonathan.

In the wake of Saul's death, the tribe of Judah takes initiative and crowns David as their king. However, there is a surviving son of Saul named Ish-bosheth ("man of shame") who reigns in the north, and a civil war between Judah and the rest of the tribes soon ensues. The leading figure in the north is Abner the military commander, and despite his subordinate status to Ish-bosheth, he is clearly calling the shots. Abner's counterpart in the south is Joab, David's nephew and the general of his army. Hostilities commence after some hand-to-hand combat goes sideways (2:12–16), and Abner's killing of Joab's brother (2:23) should be kept in mind as this conflict continues.

> *There was a long battle between the house of Saul and the house of David. David grew stronger and stronger, but the house of Saul grew weaker and weaker.* (2 Samuel 3:1)

The house of David is gaining strength from a military standpoint, and also numerically according to the list of wives and sons at the beginning of chapter 3 (although multiplying wives is a violation of Deut 17:17).

Abner's decision to betray Ish-bosheth is crucial, and perhaps he wants to be David's second-in-command, but nothing is stated on the record. However, Abner is stabbed in the ribs by Joab (3:27), officially in revenge for his brother but maybe also to eliminate this dangerous rival. Tangled motives and power plays will be a hallmark of Israel's royal story until the very end. The treacherous assassination of Ish-bosheth in chapter 4 leaves the northern tribes with few options, and soon all the elders of the north journey to the southern capital of Hebron where *they anointed David king over Israel* (5:3). Remnants of Saul's house linger for a while (e.g., chapter 9), perhaps as a harbinger of more intense conflicts between the northern tribes and southern Judah still to come.

Goliath's head was taken to Jerusalem quite some time ago, and whether David was scouting out the terrain or making a grisly down payment, his conquest of this strategically located city in chapter 5 is a pivot point in the story. The confidence of the Jebusite inhabitants is reflected in their strange taunt, but along with his private militia, David is the first Israelite to permanently capture the city. Renamed *the City of David* (5:9), Jerusalem soon becomes the political capital of the nation. The ark of the covenant is relocated to Jerusalem in chapter 6 (though not without casualties along the way), and so it also becomes the nation's spiritual center. At the end of the chapter 6 there is a disagreement with David's (first) wife Michal, and he will experience much more domestic drama before the book of 2 Samuel is over.

The astonishing divine promise announced to David in 2 Samuel 7 will carry lasting implications. The chapter begins with David in conversation with Nathan the prophet, who is introduced here for the first time. It sounds like the king wants to build a temple ("a house"), somewhat of a risky proposition given that Israel is supposed to be unique among all the peoples of the earth. Getting prophetic approval would be helpful for the king, and Nathan dutifully obliges: *all that is in your heart, go and do, for the Lord is with you* (7:3). But God overrides Nathan, and in a long oracle instructs the prophet to bring a different word to David. While God has no need for a temple—after all, he is not an insecure deity who needs a luxurious palace—he nonetheless will allow David's successor to build a temple ("a house"). More radically, David is told that *the Lord will build you a house*, and in this sense, *house* refers to a lasting dynasty. So far there have been some far-reaching promises (e.g., God's word to Abraham: "through your offspring every family on earth will be blessed"), and now here's another one:

> *Your house and your kingdom will endure before me forever, your throne will be established forever.* (2 Samuel 7:16)

The next chapters are framed by conflict with the neighboring Ammonites, and it forms a prelude to an internal conflict that nearly destroys David's reign. In the opening line of 2 Samuel 11 the Israelite army besieges a neighboring Ammonite city, *but David sat in Jerusalem*. This is the first of several ambiguities in the chapter, and David soon impregnates the wife of one of his generals, Uriah the Hittite. Summoning Uriah home, it seems as though David wants the paternity of the child to be ascribed to the legitimate father, but Uriah does return home to his wife Bathsheba (herself the granddaughter of David's prime minister, Ahithophel). Whether Uriah has any suspicions or not, in desperation David writes a letter to Joab outlining a plan for Uriah's demise, and Uriah becomes the courier of his own death warrant. Joab adjusts the king's orders, and David marries Bathsheba after Uriah is killed by the Ammonites. Ominously, the final line of the chapter (*but the thing that David had done was evil in the eyes of the Lord*; 11:27) implies that David will not get away with adultery, murder, or the subsequent cover-up.

Hour 20: 2 Samuel 12–24

NATHAN ANNOUNCED THE PROMISE of a lasting house to David in chapter 7, but at the start of chapter 12 he is sent with a different kind of message. Reacting to Nathan's story by siding against the rapacious rich man, David unintentionally condemns himself, and is unmasked when the prophet declares, *you are the man!* (12:7). The divine promise of a house that endures forever is not nullified, but a clause is now attached, as the king is told that because he took Uriah's wife and had Uriah killed with the sword, so *the sword will never depart from your house* (12:10). This is followed by the pronouncement that evil will arise out of David's house, a dire forecast that will unfold in Absalom's rebellion shortly to come. Before that, the child born to Bathsheba is struck with a mortal illness, and David is stricken with guilt. But the birth of another child also occurs, and noting the importance of a change in name, young Solomon is a character to watch in the long term:

> *She gave birth to a son, she called his name Solomon, and the Lord loved him. He sent by the hand of Nathan the prophet, and he called his name Jedidiah, because of the Lord. (2 Samuel* 12:24–25)

Amnon is listed as David's firstborn son in 2 Sam 3:2, and we might assume that he is the successor to his father's throne. But at the outset of chapter 13 Amnon is fixated on his sister Tamar (a sibling of Absalom). Nathan has just declared to David that *out of your own house evil will arise against you*, and this prophetic word starts reaching toward its grim fulfillment when David's nephew assists Amnon in a perverted scheme, by which sister Tamar is violently abused. Amnon's deed is unspeakably evil, and this scenario is eerily similar to David's conduct in chapter 11: sexual immorality soon followed by a murder. Indeed, Absalom seeks revenge for the heinous crime against Tamar, but by killing Amnon he is much closer to the throne himself. David is deceived through Absalom's patient machination in 13:23–29, and after Amnon's death Absalom flees the country to take refuge with his grandfather.

The military commander Joab does not trust Absalom in a foreign country, and tricks David into bringing him back and placing him under house arrest in chapter 14. Not only is Absalom a pyromaniac—burning Joab's field is hardly advisable—but he is also greatly admired for his beauty and has copious hair: every year he would get a haircut and weigh it, *and it was two hundred shekels by the king's measure* (14:26). Joab's fears are certainly justified as Absalom subtly seeks to displace his father. Over a long period of time he stands at the city and gradually steals the hearts of the Israelites (15:6), and when he gathers allies and the time is right, he launches his rebellion in the southern city of Hebron. David has little choice but to flee from Jerusalem, and the betrayal is complete when he is told that his chief counselor Ahithophel has joined with the rebel forces. At what must be the lowest moment of his life, he utters a desperate prayer: *please, Lord, frustrate the counsel of Ahithophel* (15:31).

Renowned for his advice, Ahithophel brutally counsels that Absalom publicly defile his father's concubines (16:20–23), and then unfolds his plan for a quick strike at the start of chapter 17, stating that he will lead a force to hunt down the king while he is weary and vulnerable. But inexplicably Absalom asks for a second opinion from David's friend Hushai, who is secretly operating as a subversive agent (noted earlier in 15:32–37). With some calculated appeals to the young man's vanity, Hushai suggests that Absalom gather a much larger force and personally lead them into battle. Not only is the advice of Hushai preferred, but Ahithophel—surely sensing the folly of this counsel and inevitable defeat—hangs himself (17:23). Much later in the New Testament a character will hang himself after betraying a descendant of the house of David (Matt 27:5).

While Absalom organizes the large-scale assault, some allies rally to David's cause on the other side of the Jordan, and at the beginning of chapter 18 David assembles his fighters (having received the covert message from Hushai). David orders his generals to *deal gently* with Absalom, the battle results in the loss of 20,000 Israelites, and *on that day the forest devoured more troops than those who were devoured by the sword* (18:8). The forest claims one more victim as Absalom is riding on his mule, because his head gets caught in the branches of an oak tree, and he is left dangling between heaven and earth. When Joab (whose barley field had previously been burned) hears about it, he finishes off Absalom, who is then buried under a pile of rocks. David is known for his poetic elegance and soaring eulogies, but upon hearing of Absalom's death he is reduced to stammering grief:

> *The king was shaken, and he went up to the roof-chamber of the gate, and wept. As he was going, he said, "My son, O Absalom, my son, my son, O Absalom! How I wish I died in place of you, O Absalom, my son, my son!"* (2 Samuel 19:1–2)

Warning the king that other disasters could follow, Joab perceives that the rebellion has opened a deep fissure, and David needs to act quickly with some damage control. The lengthy report of the king's return over the Jordan River shows some of those trouble spots, and ends on a note of unresolved quarreling. As Joab predicts, there is more conflict in chapter 20, and while the insurrection of Sheba is quashed, simmering hostilities are going to resurface later in 1 Kings.

Second Samuel 21–24 is often labeled as an appendix, with a flashback to a chilling episode involving Saul's descendants, lists of loyal warriors (including Uriah), poetic lyrics, and legendary exploits. The episode in chapter 24 involves the purchase of property that ultimately becomes the site of the Jerusalem temple in the next installment of the narrative. At the end of 2 Samuel, it might be worth noting that the journey of David (sojourn in the wilderness, establishment in the city, exile from Jerusalem, and chastened return) is similar to the journey of the larger nation in due course. The name David means *beloved*, and perhaps he is a more representative character than we may realize, as he represents the people of God and all the capacity for both remarkable faith and shocking folly. The promise of David's lasting house survives at the end of this book, but it will be further tested as the story continues.

Hour 21: 1 Kings 1–11

THE BOOKS OF 1 and 2 Kings unfold the drama of over forty monarchs, each of whom is failure in one way or another. The story of 1 Kings begins with an image of an aged and impotent David, who has not named a successor. This power vacuum triggers a struggle to claim the throne of Israel, led by the oldest surviving son, Adonijah. Inviting allies from the military and priesthood to a virtual coronation feast, it is notable that Adonijah does not invite his younger brother Solomon (1:10), but is this because he is irrelevant, or perceived as a threat?

Nathan the prophet was also not invited to Adonijah's party, and he collaborates with Bathsheba to maneuver Solomon toward the crown (with shades of Rebekah and Jacob in Genesis 27). Whether David has previously sworn an oath about Solomon's succession, Nathan and Bathsheba effectively press the claim, to the point that even while Adonijah's feast is in full swing, the announcement is made at the Gihon spring, *long live King Solomon* (1:39). Hearing the news about the anointing of a king they did not support, Adonijah's guests quickly disperse, while he takes refuge at the horns of the altar and hopes for clemency. Adonijah wants Solomon to swear an oath of guaranteeing his safety, but is only given a conditional utterance (*If he is worthy, then not one of his hairs will fall to the earth. But if evil is found in him, then he will die*), as Solomon's first words reveal him to be self-assured and cunning.

At the end of his eventful life, David's final speech at the beginning of chapter 2 has two parts. In the context of a charge to his son and successor, David emphasizes obedience and starts by exhorting Solomon to walk in the ways of the Lord *as is written in the law of Moses, in order that you may prosper in everything you do and everywhere you turn* (2:2). But the instructions take a darker turn in the second part of the speech, with advice to destroy Joab and use wisdom to circumvent the oath of Shimei and *bring down his gray head in blood to Sheol* (2:9). The deaths of Adonijah, Joab, and Shimei of Benjamin in rapid succession may well conform to David's advice, but may also give the reader an uneasy feeling. After the domestic purge of his opponents, the new king becomes a serious player on the international stage:

> *And Solomon became a son-in-law of Pharaoh king of Egypt, and he took the daughter of Pharaoh and brought her to the city of David until he finished building his house, the house of the Lord, and the wall surrounding Jerusalem.* (1 Kings 3:1)

Such an Egyptian alliance is prestigious, but also is condemned in Deuteronomy 7. Nonetheless, God gives Solomon the gift of wisdom that will never be surpassed, and it is publicly displayed when he decides a difficult case involving two prostitutes (3:16–28). Yet the king's conduct is questionable when he shifts the traditional tribal boundaries into more favorable tax districts (4:7–19), and continues the partnership with Hiram of Tyre, who earlier sent building materials to David (5:15–26). In return for vast quantities of food, Solomon gets supplies for his architectural projects, the largest of which is his palace nicknamed the *house of the forest of Lebanon* that takes thirteen years to build (7:1–2).

The reason for the palace's immense size is withheld for the moment, but more attention is devoted to the Jerusalem temple located right beside it. Much of chapters 6 and 7 detail its design, furnishings (headlined by the ark of the covenant protected by winged cherubim), and imagery evoking great memories of the past: two pillars remind us of the cloud and fire in the wilderness, pomegranates with their many seeds picture numerous offspring, and the bronze sea represents the vanquishing of chaos at both creation and the crossing of the Red Sea. Instead of a priest, King Solomon himself presides over an extensive dedication ceremony in chapter 8, with a sweeping prayer that even (ominously?) outlines provisions for a return after exile from the land because of disobedience. Unlike during he careers of Saul and David, prophets are not prominent in Solomon's reign. However, God speaks personally to the king on more than one occasion, and in chapter 9 issues a stern warning:

> *But if you or your sons surely turn away from me and do not keep my commandments or statutes which I have placed before you, and if you go after and serve other gods and bow down to them, then I will cut off Israel from the face of the ground which I gave to them. And the house that I set apart for my name I will dismiss out of my*

> *sight, such that Israel will become a proverb and a byword among the nations.* (1 Kings 9:6–7)

No reaction from Solomon is recorded, and the rest of this chapter and the next enumerate the lavish wealth and prestige of the kingdom, even attracting visits from foreign dignitaries such as the Queen of Sheba. There is also notice of land transactions with Hiram, a fleet of trading ships, and the staggering quantity of gold in Solomon's annual revenue stream (and silver was essentially worthless in Jerusalem). Mention of gold is a reminder of Deuteronomy 17:16–17, where any future king is prohibited from amassing gold, and should not acquire multiple wives nor import horses from Egypt. But not only does Solomon collect thousands of horses and chariots, he also imports horses from Egypt (10:28).

A mind-boggling unmasking occurs in chapter 11, as it is revealed that Solomon has accumulated 700 wives and 300 concubines over the years. Love, we should recognize, has nothing to do with it: these relationships represent a network of alliances and intermarriages that are contrary to the law of Moses (e.g., Deuteronomy 7:3). Moreover, on the hill opposite to Jerusalem, Solomon built worship installations for other deities such as Chemosh and Molech. Once more God speaks, this time announcing a penalty for the king's divided heart: when his son succeeds him on the throne, the kingdom will divide, with only one tribe left for the truncated house of David: *I will definitely tear the kingdom away from you and give it to your servant* (11:11).

After this announcement a *servant* is introduced, an industrious northerner named Jeroboam who had earlier been promoted by the king (11:28). Outfitted in a new coat, Jeroboam encounters the prophet Ahijah of Shiloh, who unfurls a ripping oracle. Because of Solomon's disobedience, a new kingdom will be torn away and given to Jeroboam, and if he just listens to all that *I command you, and you walk in my ways*, then God assures him that *I will build for you a lasting house, just as I built one for David, and I will give you Israel* (11:38). Somehow Solomon hears about this and tries to kill Jeroboam, who is given refuge in Egypt despite the marriage alliance of chapter 3. Jeroboam has been given an incredible promise with every opportunity to succeed, and all he has to do is walk in the right path.

Hour 22: 1 Kings 12–21

Upon the death of Solomon, his son Rehoboam moves to the foreground at the outset of chapter 12, although he has not been previously mentioned in the story. It is probably a good move for Rehoboam to venture up to Shechem and listen to the complaint of the northerners. They received harsh treatment under Solomon, but if Rehoboam lightens their taxes and workload, they will accept him as their king. Unwisely, Rehoboam rejects this offer, and within a very short time the kingdom divides, just as God forecasted in chapter 11. From now on, instead of one united people, there are two nations: Judah and the city of Jerusalem in the south, and the rest of the tribes in the north. Rehoboam barely escapes getting stoned in Shechem (12:18) and returns to Jerusalem as the king of Judah alone.

Attention turns to Jeroboam in the second half of chapter 12, who has been declared king over the breakaway northern kingdom. He has been tasked with walking in the ways of the Torah, but he quickly departs from the prophetic word of great promise. He builds golden calves in Bethel and Dan, appoints priests who are not Levites, and changes the festive calendar to discourage northerners from worshipping in Jerusalem. Chapter 13 features several prophetic confrontations that illustrate Jeroboam's waywardness, and in chapter 14 his fate is sealed. Ahijah of Shiloh is now blind, but he sees right through the disguise of Jeroboam's wife, and essentially reverses the earlier oracle. Jeroboam could have had a lasting dynasty, but now the end of his house is at hand, and he becomes the negative standard against which all other kings are measured.

From now on the style of the book of Kings features switchbacks between the southern and northern kingdoms, and as chapter 14 continues, Rehoboam returns to view. Lest the north be blamed disproportionately, 14:22–24 lists all sorts of abhorrent practices in Judah as well. Rehoboam also has to deal with an Egyptian invasion—evidently Solomon's alliance is meaningless—as Shishak marches into Jerusalem and loots the gold from the temple and palace. Even the gold shields are taken, and Rehoboam replaces them with bronze ones, visually underscoring his humiliation. When his son takes over in chapter 15, conflict with northern Israel occurs, a war that intensifies during the much longer reign of the next king of Judah. Asa clears out much of the idolatrous paraphernalia, but to aid his cause in the civil war Asa hires Ben-Hadad of Damascus. These Arameans provide some temporary assistance, but will pose a larger threat to northern Israel in due course.

Baasha in the north is one of several fruitless kings in chapter 16. A prophetic word announces his doom in 16:1–4, and soon his son Elah is toppled by his treasonous military commander Zimri, and it should be noted that Elah was drunk at the time of his assassination (16:9–10). However, the usurper Zimri makes his own questionable decisions: reigning for a total of seven days, he is then besieged by another military commander named Omri. For some reason, Zimri lights the palace on fire—while he is still in it—and not surprisingly he dies. Having seized power, Omri purchases land that becomes the city of Samaria and capital of the northern kingdom until its fall in 2 Kings 17.

Omri's son Ahab takes over as king, and becomes a dominant character in the next phase of the story. Not only does Ahab exceed all who precede him in evil, but together with his Phoenician wife Jezebel, a Baal temple—honoring the Canaanite god of storms and fertility—is built in Samaria. But there is prophetic opposition, and the next chapter begins with a sparse introduction to Elijah, who abruptly confronts the northern king: "*As the Lord God of Israel lives, before whom I stand, there will not be in these years dew or rain except at my word*" (17:1). Elijah's name means "My God is the Lord," and these opening words are a declaration of theological war, ironically undermining the assertion that Baal is the god who sends the rains. Given the danger, Elijah is divinely instructed to flee the country and take refuge in Phoenicia, of all places, Jezebel's home turf. In this foreign locale Elijah sustains a widow with food (17:8–24) and raises her son from mortal illness.

Mount Carmel is located in northwest Israel, and in chapter 18 it is the site for a showdown between Elijah and Ahab's Baal prophets after a long drought. With the indecisive Israelites watching, Elijah challenges his opponents, and when God responds by consuming the offering with fire, the people give a shout of acclamation (18:39). Rain soon follows—completing the victory—but after receiving a death threat from Jezebel at the start of chapter 19, Elijah seems depressed and ventures to Horeb, the mountain of God. Not only does the prophet experience earthquaking moments in a dark cave, but there is also a small and barely perceptible divine voice (perhaps translated *a sound of thin silence*). Elijah is also told that he will have an assistant, and Elisha (introduced in 19:19–21) soon plays an important role as he follows in his master's footsteps.

King Ahab is the center of attention in the next three chapters, including his battle with the Arameans (chapter 20) and annexing the vineyard of Naboth (chapter 21), where Elijah returns to announce the end of Ahab's house. The end of that house starts with the demise of Ahab himself, which violently unfolds in the eventful chapter 22. For whatever purpose, Jehoshaphat king of Judah forms an alliance with Ahab, and therefore is obligated to join his northern counterpart in an attack against the foreign outpost of Ramoth-Gilead. But the prophet Micaiah forecasts a personal disaster for Ahab (22:17–23), who tries to outmaneuver this dire word by disguising himself during the battle. These elaborate measures are futile, because when an Aramean soldier draws his bow at random and shoots an arrow, it just happens to strike Ahab right between the joints of his armor.

> *He shouted to his charioteer, "Turn your hand, get me out of the camp, for I am wounded!" The battle heightened on that day, with the king being propped up on his chariot opposite Aram. In the evening he died, as the blood of the wound poured out into the heart of the chariot.* (1 Kings 22:34–35)

Elijah had earlier declared that *dogs* will lap up the blood of Ahab (21:19), and when the blood-soaked chariot is rinsed out after Ahab's death, the *dogs* are ready and start lapping (22:38). Ahab built an ivory palace, but his descendants will not live there for too much longer. Ahab's dynasty will not endure, although Jezebel remains in the storyline until 2 Kings 9. Near the end of chapter 22, Jehoshaphat's career is summarized, and a notable event is a maritime disaster. This report is metaphorically fitting, since he nearly shipwrecks the southern kingdom because of his alliance with Ahab.

Hour 23: 2 Kings 1–13

AHAZIAH IS THE SUCCESSOR to Ahab, but suffers a calamitous fall as 2 Kings opens. Instead of entreating the God of Israel, Ahaziah provokes the fiery wrath of Elijah by seeking Baal-zebub ("lord of the flies") without effectiveness. Meanwhile, there are rumors circulating about Elijah's impending departure as chapter 2 opens, and a group called *the sons of the prophets* variously appear. This group seems to have arisen to counter the ideology of Ahab's house, and aims to keep the prophetic word alive in dark times. Elisha gets a double portion of his master's spirit when he sees Elijah transported to the divine realm in a chariot of fire. He then begins his own journey, by healing the waters of Jericho followed by a ferocious episode with the bears of Bethel at the end of chapter 2.

The various deeds of Elisha form a compelling message that urges the Israelites to return to God, and his busy northern itinerary implies that time is slowly running out. Chapters 3 and 4 feature miracles of water and food alongside healing and resurrection, continuing and enhancing the work of his predecessor Elijah. An extended episode of cleansing the Aramean commander Naaman from leprosy underscores God's sovereignty beyond the borders of Israel in chapter 5, and when the same Arameans lay siege to Samaria in the next scenes, God's capacity to feed and rescue are highlighted again. Four lepers stumble into an abandoned enemy camp, and their collective conscience ("*What we are doing is not right! Today is a day of good news . . . come, let's go tell the king's house!*") compels them to share this astounding discovery with the beleaguered city (7:9).

Nearing the end of his career, Elisha also ventures into foreign territory and tearfully converses with a foreign usurper, Hazael of Damascus (8:7–15). This provides a grim preview of numerous invasions as the book continues. Hazael is mentioned again in 8:28, when it is revealed that Judah's king Ahaziah has also been entangled with northern Israel *because he was a son-in-law to the house of Ahab*. Ahaziah goes to visit the northern king, and it will prove to be a fateful decision in the next chapter. Indeed, at the beginning of 2 Kings 9 Elisha commissions a young prophetic figure to secretly anoint a military general named Jehu as king (referred in 1 Kings 19:16, along with Hazael). Jehu's crowning ignites the uprising that finally brings the curtain down on the house of Ahab—with consequences for southern Judah as well, since they are part of this problematic alliance. When Jehu's fellow officers find out about the anointing, the conspiracy against the Ahab dynasty is officially launched:

> *Each man quickly took his cloak to place it under Jehu on the steps of the stairway. They sounded the trumpet and declared, "Jehu reigns!"* (2 Kings 9:13)

Jehu sets off to eradicate the house of Ahab, and his violent purge is foreshadowed by some wild chariot driving (9:20), for which he apparently has a reputation. Both kings are in the same place, Jezreel, and in short order both kings are assassinated as they meet up with Jehu at Naboth's vineyard: Ahab's son is shot first with an arrow from Jehu's bow in 9:24, followed soon by Ahaziah of Judah, who is likewise pierced by an arrow and dies in 9:27. Jehu then encounters Jezebel in 9:30–37, who is duly thrown from a window after arranging her hair and uttering an ironic reference to Zimri (1 Kings 16:18), the hapless usurper who reigned for a mere seven days.

Seventy descendants of Ahab remain in Samaria, but Jehu sends intimidating letters to their governors at the beginning of chapter 10. Gripped with fear, the governors proceed to destroy the princes themselves, and after Jehu's further rampage on his journey to Samaria, the house of Ahab is completely destroyed. Jehu turns his sights to the Baal temple in the second half of chapter 10: pretending to host a grand sacrifice (*Ahab served Baal a little, Jehu will serve him more!*), Jehu assembles all the leading dignitaries of Baal worship, replete with robes, as the place is filled from end to end. There is a sacrifice, but it is the Baal leaders who are put to the sword, and the temple is flattened: *They smashed the pillar of Baal, and tore down the house of Baal and turned it into a latrine until this day* (10:27). But after reigning for nearly three decades, Jehu dies with a negative evaluation, having not been careful to adhere to the teaching of the Lord.

Meanwhile, a very dark interval unfolds in southern Judah. In the aftermath of Jehu's violence, chapter 11 starts with Athaliah—Jezebel's daughter in all likelihood—stepping into the power vacuum left in Jerusalem when her son is killed by the arrow. She proceeds to massacre the royal offspring, which would include her own family, nearly obliterating the line of David. But her daughter secretly rescues the infant prince Joash, hiding him in the temple for seven years while Athaliah rules the land of Judah. During this period, the priest Jehoiada orchestrates a palace coup (11:4–16) that results in the execution of Athaliah and a coronation ceremony for the young Joash. The Davidic line is restored with the crowning of Joash, and chapter 12 outlines his forty-year reign, including his efforts to refurbish the temple and payments to offset an invasion by Hazael of Damascus. A conspiracy brings Joash to the throne, but another conspiracy ends his career when his own courtiers later plot against him (12:21–22).

Not mentioned since Jehu's anointing, Elisha the prophet makes a surprising comeback in chapter 13 as the story switches to the north, where a grandson of Jehu reigns in Samaria (v. 10). A word is sought from Elisha, and the prophet forecasts that the king will drive back the Arameans three times, but it could have been greater (suggesting a halfhearted commitment of the king). But the last act is incredible, for just as Elijah had an unprecedented exit from the narrative stage replete with chariots of fire, so Elisha has his own memorable cameo:

> *Elisha died, and they buried him. Now raiding parties of Moab would enter the land during the spring season. Once as they were burying a man, behold, they saw the raiding party, and threw the man in the grave of Elisha. The man went down, touched the bones of Elisha, lived, and arose to his feet.* (2 Kings 13:20–21)

In the next installments of the story the nation will be thrown into the graves of exile. Perhaps the message of this anecdote is an encouragement for future generations to have confidence in the life-infusing power of the prophetic word. As Elisha's bones can revive the dead, maybe there will be hope for the nation to once again be restored to the land and have a chance to reconsider *the covenant with Abraham, Isaac, and Jacob* (13:23).

Hour 24: 2 Kings 14–25

In the last half of 2 Kings there is a relentless march toward invasion, destruction, and exile, and tellingly, a main event of chapter 14 is a costly civil war between Israel and Judah. Entanglement with northern Israel is a disaster that Judah could have avoided, and ends with a looted temple and prisoners (not for the last time). In 14:23–29 Jeroboam II reigns in Samaria, and reclaims territory in alignment with the prophetic prompting of Jonah. But a rapid turnover of northern regimes is noted in the next chapter, and it coincides with the official notice of Assyria in the storyline (15:19). Encroachment into the land by this vicious superpower requires substantial payment, necessitating heavy taxation. With the Assyrian presence increasingly reported in the text, there will be devastating implications for both north and south.

The high price of the Assyrian advance is most noticeable with Ahaz of Judah in chapter 16. Alongside a listing of his abhorrent practices, Ahaz also makes a deal with Assyria to offset pressure from an alliance between Samaria and Damascus. But it is a costly arrangement, and after the fall of Damascus a subservient Ahaz imports Assyrian religious practices and a refabricated altar into the heart of the Jerusalem temple. In the end, Ahaz's deferential strategy of appeasement will prove ineffective, as his successor Hezekiah (16:20) shortly discovers. The last northern king, Hoshea, is likewise a vassal to Assyria, but is caught in an act of treachery (17:4) that leads to a three-year siege of Samaria, with the population eventually dispersed and new people groups brought in. Much of chapter 17 is a very long indictment, as the curtain lifts and a litany of abuses are catalogued:

> *The Lord was very angry with Israel and turned them away from his presence. Only the tribe of Judah remained. But even Judah did not keep the commands of the Lord their God, for they walked in the practices of Israel. The Lord rejected all the descendants of Israel; he*

> *afflicted them and gave them into the hands of plunderers, until he threw them from his presence.* (2 Kings 17:18–20)

Against the backdrop of the northern kingdom's smoldering ruins, Assyria moves southward with Judah and Jerusalem as the next target. The reign of Hezekiah is better than most, and even though he makes a massive payment to the Assyrians (18:15), their field commander arrives at the wall of the Jerusalem with a menacing speech in the second half of chapter 18. In desperation Hezekiah goes to the temple to pray (19:1), and in due course receives a long oracle from the prophet Isaiah with an unlikely forecast: God declares that the king of Assyria will not enter Jerusalem, *for I will defend this city in order to save it, for my sake and for the sake of David my servant* (19:34). Early the next morning, the citizens see 185,000 dead soldiers as Isaiah's word is fulfilled, while the Assyrian king is assassinated by his sons after returning home to Nineveh. As for Hezekiah, he receives another prophetic utterance from Isaiah after entertaining some Babylonian diplomats who offer congratulations on his recovery from illness (20:1–13). But this time Isaiah's forecast is entirely grim, as he announces that the Babylonians will one day return only to carry off everything of value (20:17–18). Even though Jerusalem survives the Assyrian advance, it sounds like the beginning of the end.

Manasseh's fifty-five-year reign in 2 Kings 21 breaks a couple of records, for not only does he have the longest tenure, but he also achieves the highest level of apostasy as he builds altars for all the hosts of heaven (v. 4) alongside sculptured images of the goddess Asherah that he places in the temple (v. 7). His dismal resumé includes divination and child sacrifice, prompting God to speak through the prophets in the harshest terms through a long oracle declaring that Jerusalem's citizens will become *plunder and prey to all their enemies* (21:14). By contrast, Manasseh's grandson Josiah receives a much better rating in chapters 22–23, and a crucial moment is his humble response to a reading of the book of the law that was "found" (or was it hidden during the dark years of Manasseh?). But Josiah's energetic reforms and celebration of the Passover (23:21) are not enough to avert the forthcoming disaster. Although Josiah is surely one of the best kings of Judah, his premature death in battle is an ominous prelude to the final countdown.

Isaiah had warned that Babylon would return, and the onslaught is unleashed in chapter 24 as Nebuchadnezzar's soldiers seize control of all the land from the wadi of Egypt to the Euphrates, territory that was once long ago governed by Solomon (1 Kings 4:21). Young Jehoiachin is carried off to Babylon along with other leading citizens and warriors (24:12–16), and replaced with Zedekiah, his uncle. Under Zedekiah's watch, the city of Jerusalem falls in chapter 25. After an eighteen-month siege the wall is pierced, and Zedekiah tries vainly to escape, only to be captured and have his eyes gouged out after watching the execution of his sons (25:7).

While Zedekiah is marched into oblivion, the houses of Jerusalem are burned and the temple is bulldozed: several long chapters described the building of the temple, but in a sad contrast, a very short paragraph reports how it is dismantled and looted (25:13–17). The poorest are left behind, yet are soon the victims of Ishmael's (from the royal family) treachery, and flee to Egypt. Many others are sent into exile and dispersed into various Babylonian provinces. Back in Genesis 12 Abraham leaves this same area and walks to Canaan because of God's promise, but now his descendants reverse the journey in a long walk of shame.

But after the dust settles on this most traumatic sequence of events, the book finishes with an unexpected moment. Not seen since his own march into captivity in chapter 24, Jehoiachin briefly returns to the stage as the object of imperial favor. He had been humiliatingly taken into captivity as a teenager, but the narrative closes with this Davidic heir having a place at the emperors' table:

> *He spoke kindly toward him, and placed his seat higher than the other kings who were with him in Babylon. Then Jehoiachin changed his prison clothes, and continually dined before him all the days of his life.* (2 Kings 25:28–29)

Several elements in this concluding scene—such as royal favor and new clothes—are reminiscent of the Joseph story, suggesting a more hopeful set of possibilities. Jehoiachin is a surviving member of the house of David, and even if the story is dangling at the end, it implies that the fulfillment of the promise to David about a lasting house is still in the cards, despite the catalogue of misdeeds and recent horrors. The next book in the Hebrew Bible is the great scroll of Isaiah, where further prophetic words about the future of the Davidic house can be heard, and instead of the end, the exile will bring about a new beginning.

Hour 25: Isaiah 1–39

As we recall, the prophet Isaiah has a memorable role in 2 Kings 19–20, during the height of the Assyrian advance against Judah. Approaching the book of Isaiah after reading 2 Kings now provides an "insider's view," that is, a prophetic perspective on a variety of events and figures. Indeed, the opening superscription locates Isaiah during the turbulent period around the reign of Hezekiah, but as is soon apparent, the prophetic word unfolds against the backdrop of several imperial powers. So far in the Hebrew Bible we have predominantly been dealing with narrative material, but the book of Isaiah is mainly poetry, and the reader is invited to linger over the wealth of images that are presented. Like other great art forms, poetry engages the imagination in order to invite an audience to new places, and to provide an immersive experience amidst the tumult and chaos of this historical period, along with a fresh vision of the divine character.

Isaiah's message in chapter 1 begins with the heavens and earth called as a witness to hear an indictment against a rebellious nation, a *people loaded with guilt* who *offer meaningless sacrifices* (1:3–4). The consequences for such disobedience will be severe (*your cities burned with fire, fields devoured by strangers*, 1:7), but also with assurances of a later rehabilitation: *you will be called the city of righteousness, a faithful city* (1:26). A sequence of oracles in chapter 2–5 interweaves warnings of judgment (e.g., *the eyes of the arrogant will be humbled*, 2:11; *grinding the faces of the poor*, 3:15; *my people will go into exile for lack of understanding*, 5:12) with glimpses of hope in the aftermath of catastrophe (e.g., *on that day the mountain of the Lord's temple will be established, and all nations will stream to it*, 2:2; *in that day the branch of Lord the will be beautiful and glorious*, 4:2). The climactic scene of the opening section is Isaiah's commissioning in chapter 6, and despite initial hesitation, his unclean lips are purified and he is sent to a wayward people to declare a message that will not be received:

> *In the year King Uzziah died, I saw the Lord seated on a throne, high and lifted up, with the train of his robe filling the temple. Seraphs* ["fiery ones"] *were stationed above him . . .* (Isaiah 6:1–2)

Ahaz of Jerusalem is confronted by Isaiah in chapter 7, but does not seem interested in receiving such prophetic counsel. Tensions have increased because of an alliance between northern Israel (sometimes called "Ephraim") and Damascus, who have united against Assyria and are threatening to depose Ahaz unless he joins their coalition. A mysterious sign about a pregnant young woman is given to the king, and before the child (the name *Immanuel* means "God with us"; later cited in Matthew 1:23) is old enough to determine right from wrong, both Damascus and northern Israel will be shattered. In 8:3 Isaiah's wife makes an appearance, and their children bear symbolic names that forecast the coming disaster on Judah at the hands of the Assyrians whom Ahaz is tempted to trust. Yet in the wake of catastrophe, there are visions of another royal child on whose shoulders the government will rest, and he will be called *everlasting father* and *prince of peace* (9:6). From the line of David (11:1–10), this figure is part of a movement to regather those who have been dispersed, and there will be great cause for celebration (12:4).

Many of the prophetic books include oracles to foreign peoples, and chapters 13–23 unfurl a collection of various words (or "burdens") for the nations. Instead of a linear plot line, a movement back and forth in time creates a tapestry of images. Babylon is at the top of this list in 13–14, the superpower whose shadow is cast especially over the second half of the book. For all its pomp and splendor, this nation will be brought down to the grave (14:11) and swept away with the broom of destruction (14:23). Oracles follow against places like Assyria, Moab, Damascus, and Egypt, culminating with a notice that the extravagant wealth of Tyre will have a market crash when *the fortress of the sea* (23:4–13) is turned into a ruin. Whether these compositions were supposed to be delivered to the nations is uncertain, but they are certainly intended for Israel's reflection, illustrating how the sovereignty of God towers above every empire and the swirling vortex of current events.

The horizon of Isaiah's vision continues to expand in chapters 24–27, a poetic sequence that further emphasizes the theme of restoration after chaos. It begins with a vision of God laying waste the earth and making it desolate (*the land is polluted by its inhabitants*, 24:5), but ends with the picture of a magnificent vineyard that replenishes the earth with fruit in 27:2–6. The oracles of chapters 28–35 both enhance and narrow this theme, with words of judgment directed toward individual and social corruptions in Israel and Judah, ranging from inauthentic worship (29:13) to misplaced confidence in alliances with nations like Egypt (31:1–3). Harrowing scenes of divine wrath poured out against antagonistic Edomites and *the sky rolled up like a scroll* (34:4) then give way to a stunning tableau in the next chapter, with a blooming desert and streams in the barren wasteland. As though it is a new exodus, there will be a highway through the wilderness that allows God's banished people to return to the land:

> *Then those who the Lord has ransomed will return, and will arrive in Zion with ringing songs. Everlasting joy is upon their heads. Rejoicing and joy will overcome them, as sorrow and mourning have fled away.* (Isaiah 35:10)

With some slight variations, chapters 36–39 recount the Assyrian crisis that has already been narrated in 2 Kings. After the vision in chapter 35 about the redeemed exiles returning home, this section in Isaiah 36–39 is a stark reminder of how they got there. The audience experiences afresh the ferocity of the Assyrian army that has just decimated the north, and then marches south toward Jerusalem, embodied in the threatening rhetoric of the field commander. Hezekiah's helplessness in the temple is revisited, along with the inconceivable utterance of Isaiah to the Assyrian king: "*I will cause you to turn back, on the same road by which you came*" (37:29). A major purpose for repeating this episode, then, is to enhance confidence in the prophetic word as opposed to the intimidating voices of the empire. Such confidence will be desperately needed in the next installment of the book of Isaiah.

But a different view of Hezekiah also emerges in this section, and for the first time we hear his own words through his prayer of 38:9–20 in response to his deliverance from mortal illness, commemorating his life that was saved from the pit of destruction with acts of grace that *fathers will recount to their children*. However, this prayer stands as a starkly ironic introduction to his ill-advised hospitality to the Babylonians in chapter 39, which not only emphasizes their menacing presence but also forms a backdrop to Isaiah's message about the inevitable Babylonian return and Hezekiah's children becoming servants in a foreign king's palace. So, this section provides a transition to part two, the sequel of Isaiah 40–66 where exile is a grim reality. After the foreboding end of chapter 39, an agonizing and harsh silence is imagined, but then the sequel begins abruptly with a stirring pronouncement.

Hour 26: Isaiah 40–66

THE READER IS SEEMINGLY transported into a different dimension of time and space when entering the second part of the book of Isaiah. At the end of chapter 39, Hezekiah is warned that Babylon will be back to empty the treasury of Jerusalem and carry its inhabitants into captivity. Now, in part two, the reader experiences what such captivity feels like: the city's devastation is a haunting memory, and the community faces myriad problems stuck in a foreign land, deeply in need of a prophetic word of hope for the future and instruction for the present. There is no personal appearance of the prophet in this sequel. Instead, the reader hears a chorus of prophetic voices that invite the community to reconceptualize faith in God in a radically different situation. If we imagine an interval of silence between chapters 39 and 40, the silence ends as chapter 40 opens with a divine declaration that their days of hard service in exile are over: *Comfort, comfort my people, says your God.* Furthermore, the highway glimpsed in 35:8–10 is now ready for construction, and the Babylonians who seemed so unbeatable are now poised to fade like the grass of the field. This opening chapter variously describes the character of God without rival or peer, who both stretches out the vast universe and energizes a community weakened by despair:

> *Those who wait on the Lord will renew their strength, they will rise up on wings like eagles. They will run but not get weary, they will walk but not grow faint.* (Isaiah 40:31)

Restoration after the exile is a major thematic thrust of chapters 40–48, reflected in declarations such as 42:7 that express the divine intention *to bring out prisoners from the dungeon, from the house of confinement those who sit in darkness*. Liberation from Babylon will occur on multiple levels, including release from the iron grip of Babylonian ideology and the delusional idols that are images of wind and confusion (41:29). A courtroom drama plays out in this section, with a lawsuit against the idols replete with satire (44:9–20), leading to the verdict that they are unable to rescue and cannot save from distress (46:1–7). Lawsuit language is used early in chapter 1, between God and Israel. But in the second part of Isaiah the litigation is expanded to include the gods of the nations. On the political side, a key instrument of liberation is Cyrus of Persia, called the *anointed* in 45:1 and the one whom God enables to subdue nations. Babylon's fate is sealed (*evil will come upon you, and you will not know how to conjure it away*, 47:11), and Israel is to be released through the actions of God's chosen ally against Babylon (48:14–15).

Another player in this prophetic drama of restoration is a *servant*, mentioned in chapter 42 in reference to the people of Israel, but emerging with more individual prominence in chapters 49–55. Often referred to as the *suffering* servant, there is no clear indication when the servant will arise, but it does sound like this figure will be part of a remnant who bring light to the nations and who trust in the name of the Lord according to the "songs" in 49:1–6 and 50:4–11. The most influential text is 52:13–53:12, a complex oracle that features several interlocking sections. On the one hand, the servant will be despised and rejected, as well as bear the sins and crimes of a multitude: *we all like sheep have wandered astray, each of us turning to our own way, but the Lord has caused the iniquity of us all to fall on him* (53:6). On the other hand, through his suffering the servant will make many people righteous (53:11), and a large crowd will benefit by means of this sacrifice. In the New Testament these passages are applied to the life and death of Jesus (e.g., Matthew 8:17; Acts 8:32–35). Meanwhile, chapter 55 echoes earlier calls to *seek God while he can be found*, and provides a transition to the final section of the book.

The concluding section in chapters 56–66 addresses a situation where the Jerusalem temple seems to have been rebuilt and some members of the community have returned to the land. The city walls have been repaired, sacrifices are being offered, and references to the sabbath paint a picture of restoration as anticipated in the earlier oracles of Isaiah. But there are challenges that face the people in the aftermath of exile, and they evidently are beset with economic, spiritual, and leadership problems. In the midst of hardships, these oracles variously encourage the community to wholeheartedly embrace the responsibility of covenant life by continuing to reject idolatry (57:3–13) and walking in the way of peace (59:1–15). Return from exile was only the beginning, and so instead of despair, the people should imagine new contours of salvation in the days ahead:

> *Arise, shine, for your light has come, and the Lord's glory has risen upon you! For behold, darkness is covering the earth, and the peoples are in deep gloom. But the Lord will rise upon you, and his glory will be seen upon you. Then nations will come to your light, and kings to the brightness of your dawn.* (Isaiah 60:1–3)

Jerusalem is personified in the poetry of chapter 60, which emphasizes a reversal that will occur: previously, kings came to invade Jerusalem, but now they arrive as submissive vassals. Instead of emptying the treasuries and knocking down the walls, foreigners repair the infrastructure and the wealth of nations flows into Zion (60:11–14). An individual prophetic voice speaks at the outset of chapter 61 and continues the sequence of reversals (*the Lord has anointed me to carry good news to the afflicted, to tend the wounds of the brokenhearted*), while the summons to build another highway in chapter 62 anticipates that the city will experience further transformation. A collage of images and a longing prayer (*Oh that you would tear open the heavens and come down*, 64:1) set the stage for an astounding vision of renewal in chapter 65. God responds with an announcement that is later rebooted in Revelation 21, and here signals the divine intention, that, despite waywardness, includes a tacit invitation to be part of God's vast and dynamic design:

> *For behold, I am creating a new heavens and a new earth,*
> *and the previous things will not be remembered nor even come to mind.*
> *So be glad and rejoice forever in what I am creating,*
> *since I am about to create Jerusalem as a source of joy, and its people as a delight.*
> *I will rejoice in Jerusalem, and delight in my people,*
> *the noise of weeping won't be heard in it, nor any cry of distress.*
> *(Isaiah 65:17–19)*

The last chapter of the book of Isaiah returns to the theme of the temple, with a reminder of its makeshift purpose (*the heavens are my throne and the earth is my footstool*, 66:1) and a vision of a multitude swelling its precincts (18–21). Remarkably, even gentiles might be involved in leading worship and teaching God's word in the future, and not only authorized Levites. But just as the book of Isaiah begins with a challenge in chapter 1, so it ends with a warning in chapter 66 to take the divine word seriously and avoid the perilous path of unfaithfulness.

Hour 27: Jeremiah 1–26

In terms of word count, Jeremiah is the longest of the prophetic books. Jeremiah's career unfolds during the chaotic period that we read about in 2 Kings 22–25, when the nation of Judah and the city of Jerusalem are eventually devastated by the Babylonians. During the intense period leading up to the siege—followed by the demolition of the temple and the exile—the prophetic work of Jeremiah takes place. Compared with Isaiah, the reader learns much more about Jeremiah personally, and indeed, journeys with him from his younger days all the way to the end, often punctuated with unfiltered honesty and complaints voiced directly to God. But amidst some of the most trying and traumatic of circumstances, Jeremiah is also the conduit of some astonishing words of promise and consolation.

The opening lines of the book indicate that Jeremiah is active during the reigns of Judah's last five kings, from the days of Josiah's reform until the final countdown of the nation's demise. He is from a priestly family that lives in Anathoth, a village just north of Jerusalem, and itself a reminder of Abiathar's banishment in 2 Kings 2:27 because of the crimes of the priestly house of Eli (see 1 Samuel 2). If Jeremiah is a member of the doomed line of Eli, then he is personally acquainted with prophetic censure. Yet the opening chapter also reveals how Jeremiah is chosen by God: *Before I handcrafted you in the womb, I knew you* (1:5). Similar to Isaiah, Jeremiah is commissioned to be a prophet, and similar to Moses (Exodus 3), he resists the divine call by claiming that he is young and not a good speaker. God's lengthy response outlines some key thematic contours that recur throughout this long prophetic book: there will be much *uprooting*, but also some *replanting*. So, despite the carnage and dismantling, new growth and rebuilding will emerge from the ashes. Like Jerusalem itself, Jeremiah will be under siege and his own people are going to fight against him, but the divine presence is assured:

> *Behold, today I have made you as a fortified city, an iron pillar, and a bronze wall against all the land: the kings of Judah, its princes, its priests, and the people of the land. They will fight against you, but they will not prevail against you, because I am with you, declares the Lord, to deliver you.* (Jeremiah 1:18–19)

Aside from any doubts Jeremiah may have expressed about his prophetic call, the passionate oracles of chapters 2–6 begin with a poetic recounting of the exodus and journey through the wilderness, as God has brought the Israelites through a dreadful place to a land of abundance (2:6). But the people have been unfaithful: northern Israel has been cast aside, and southern Judah has not heeded this warning (3:8). There is a call to repentance in the face of coming disaster from the north (4:15), and admonition to no longer stray from the ancient path of the Torah (6:16).

For someone who claims not to know how to speak, there is evidence to the contrary, and the brave word Jeremiah is directed to proclaim at the gate of the temple in chapter 7 is a prime example. If this speech is delivered around the time of Josiah's reform or just afterwards, then temple-worship would have been fashionable after a long period of decline during the tenures of Manasseh and Amon (see 2 Kings 21). But in this high traffic area, the citizens of Judah are told that even though they are attending the temple, they are not attending to basic matters of covenant faithfulness or social justice. As a result, Jerusalem is on the verge of becoming like Shiloh (7:14), the former spiritual capital of the nation that presumably was destroyed in the days of Eli. The population is accused of secretly worshipping a goddess called the Queen of Heaven (v. 18), and consistently rejecting the message of the prophets whom God has sent (vv. 25–26). Continuing these themes, the oracles of chapters 8–10 give further warnings that a storm is brewing:

> *Gather all your belongings from the land, all of you who are living under siege, for thus says the Lord: Behold, I'm about to sling away all the inhabitants of the land at this moment. I will bring trouble on them and they will be found out.* (Jeremiah 10:17–18)

In 11:6 the prophet is told to proclaim *all these things* throughout the cities of Judah and Jerusalem's streets. Combined with his words at the gate of the temple, his own relatives from Anathoth are angry and conspire to silence him (11:19). When this plot is revealed to him, Jeremiah pours out a lament and protests his fate, questioning God about why *the way of wicked* prospers while he is the victim of treachery (12:1–4). God's response in the rest of chapter 12 is not exactly warm and comfortable, but rather an outline of how things are going to get worse, and the prophet will face even greater challenges ahead.

No verbal response from Jeremiah is recorded, but he obviously accepts God's challenge because the next sequence of the book feature prophetic "signs." These are dramatic enactments, almost like street theater, that are used to communicate the message. Examples include a linen belt in chapter 13, as the prophet buries and later retrieves a linen garment at the Euphrates River to symbolize the defilement of exile. Furthermore, *the potter's house* in chapter 18 becomes an occasion to observe a clay jar that is rejected by the artist, only to be remolded into another one in its place. In the next chapter the images of clay and smashed jars are enhanced, underlining the doom that is at hand. To this point in the book there have been plenty of allusions to the forthcoming invasion of the foe from the north, but Babylon itself is first mentioned during a confrontation with a temple officer named Pashur in chapter 20. Pashur has Jeremiah beaten and arrested, but the next day hears a chilling word:

> *For thus says the Lord: Behold, I'm about to make you a terror to yourself and to all your friends. They will fall by the sword of their enemies while your eyes look on, and all Judah I will give into the hand of the king of Babylon. He will take them as captives to Babylon, and will strike them with the sword.* (Jeremiah 20:4)

This ominous word is spoken publicly, but in private Jeremiah has inner turmoil to the point that he curses the day of his birth (20:14). Nevertheless, he endures, although confrontations continue in chapter 26 where he is nearly put to death. Jeremiah holds out the option that if each one turns from their wicked ways, then God will relent from sending calamity (26:3), but otherwise the city is on the way to becoming like Shiloh (26:6) with echoes of the earlier temple sermon. When the officials impose the death sentence, Jeremiah is rescued through an intervention by some of the elders (26:17) and a faithful group of influential supporters (including the family of Shaphan; 26:24). At the end of chapter 26 is a short anecdote about the prophet Uriah, who declares a similar prophetic word and is killed despite fleeing to Egypt. Jeremiah's career has a similar trajectory, but his life will be preserved even through the disasters in the second half of the book.

Hour 28: Jeremiah 27–52

To THIS POINT THE reader has seen some personal glimpses of Jeremiah's inner prophetic life against a backdrop of increasing anxiety and chaos as the Babylonians approach, and political factions are increasingly noticeable. We have already observed that prophetic books do not always follow a strictly linear plotline, but can be organized in a more thematic fashion. A particular stress point in the second part of this book is competition with other religious leaders, and a confrontation with Hananiah in chapter 28 provides a snapshot of the prophetic battle going on. Hananiah optimistically trumpets that Babylonian supremacy is temporary and relief is imminent, whereas Jeremiah (after some initial sarcasm in v. 6) insists that terrible times are coming. He follows up with a letter in chapter 29 addressed to those who have already been deported to Babylon, stating that they should expect to be there for a long time.

These are surely the bleakest of times in Jerusalem's history, but at the beginning of chapter 30 Jeremiah is told by God to write in a book all the words that have been spoken to him. While there is a reiteration of some very dismal news indeed (*Look, the tempest of the Lord! Wrath is marching out as a sweeping storm that bursts on the head of the wicked,* 30:23), such dire forecasts are offset by promises of restoration even as the present world crumbles. Arguably the most influential oracle is the articulation of a new covenant—the very title "New Testament" is taken from the prophetic promise in chapter 31—as God announces a forthcoming era where fresh guidance and forgiveness are hallmarks:

> *For this is the covenant I will cut with the house of Israel after those days, declares the Lord: I will put my law within them and write it on their hearts. I will be their God, and they will be my people.* (Jeremiah 31:33)

A sequence of episodes in chapters 32–39 open a window on the last hours of Judah's kingdom, with scenes filtered mainly through Jeremiah's experiences of imprisonment and antagonism. In chapter 32 he buys a piece of real estate from his cousin to illustrate that after Jerusalem's fall there will be a repopulation, while in chapter 35 the roaming Rechabites are faithful to their ancestral commitments and act as a foil to the fickle population of Judah. A main character in chapter 36 is a *scroll*, tossed in the fire by the dreadful King Jehoiakim, and although he methodically burns the scroll, the words will endure. In chapter 38 Jeremiah is thrown into an empty cistern, but rescued by the intervention of a foreign official named Ebed-Melech. This harrowing scene is followed by an extended interview with the vacillating Zedekiah, whose court is divided by warring factions. The last monarch to reign in Jerusalem, Zedekiah's attempt to flee in chapter 39 is thwarted with his arrest by the Babylonians, who march him into oblivion as the captured city smolders in ruins.

Imperial officers of Babylon do, however, give Jeremiah a choice to either journey into exile or remain behind with a meager remnant in the land. With Jeremiah deciding to stay, the narrative in chapters 40–45 reveals that even though the citizens of Judah have been humbled in defeat, the same rebellious streak remains intact. This turbulent section of the book outlines how a calamitous series of events result in treachery and assassination, and in the end Jeremiah is dragged off to Egypt by his own people (chapter 43). The prophet who spent his career imploring the Israelites to return to the God who brought them out of slavery in Egypt is now taken as a virtual captive to the same place, where he eventually fades from view, yet actively proclaiming the divine word until the end in chapter 44.

Jeremiah's career seems to finish in the sadly ironic circumstances of Egypt, but the book is not over, and chapters 46–51 include a series of oracles to the nations (compare Isaiah 13–23). Placed near the conclusion, these oracles illustrate the multinational dimension of Jeremiah's poetry that he was preaching all along, and bring the reader full circle to his call narrative at the outset when he is set apart as a *prophet to the nations* (1:5). Moreover, despite his captivity in Egypt at the end, his words have a life of their own. Starting with a message to Egypt in chapter 47, the various oracles are directed to the Philistines, Moab, Ammon, Edom, Damascus, Kedar and Hazor, and the Elamites. The longest and most complex oracle is addressed to Babylon in chapters 50–51, and although Jeremiah consistently maintained that the people of Judah should understand the Babylonian invasion as a divine discipline, this harsh nation will themselves experience some serious divine judgment:

> *The earth will quake and tremble, because the Lord's purposes against Babylon will arise, for the land of Babylon will be made a desolation, where there is no inhabitant.* (Jeremiah 51:29)

Unusually, this oracle is hand-delivered by Seraiah, the brother of Jeremiah's assistant, Baruch (see chapter 45). Seraiah is given instructions to read the words aloud, and then tie a stone to the scroll and throw it into the Euphrates River to symbolize the termination of Babylon's empire (51:59–64). The book could well finish on this note, but instead, chapter 52 provides a variation of 2 Kings 25, prompting us to wonder why this material is included as a conclusion. The last scenes in the book recount (again) the position of the exiled King Jehoiachin in the palace of Babylon. Because Jehoiachin is a descendant of David, the reader may recall earlier words of Jeremiah about the promise of David's enduring house. For example, earlier in the book there is an announcement about a time when God will raise up *a righteous branch*, and this descendant of David will rule with insight and justice in the land (23:10). The fleeting reference to David's house at the end of chapter 52 is a reminder that there is a future beyond the ravages of exile. An audience is therefore left with hope that is based on the divine word that Jeremiah has faithfully proclaimed at a costly price, and in the midst of such personal sorrow.

Hour 29: Ezekiel 1–24

The third major prophetic scroll is the book of Ezekiel, named after the main character who is a younger contemporary of Jeremiah. But during the same tumultuous period, these two figures end up at opposite ends of the map: Jeremiah is taken by his own people to Egypt near the end of his life, whereas Ezekiel is taken into early exile with Jehoiachin by the Babylonians about a decade before the invasion of Jerusalem (see 2 Kings 24:12–15). As we recall, Jeremiah's family had a dubious past, whereas Ezekiel is part of a distinguished priestly line. But when he ends up as a captive in Babylon, he now has to figure out: does God matter in this defiled foreign land, and is there any chance for Israel in the future? How can I serve God without the temple? Is God relevant now that I am in a hostile place where other powers have jurisdiction?

An opening vision in chapter 1 responds to such questions in mesmerizing way. The vision occurs by the Kebar River, probably an irrigation canal dug by slave labor (see "the rivers of Babylon" in Psalm 137). It sounds like Ezekiel is thirty years old, and according to Numbers 4:3 that would be the age that he is supposed to be commissioned for priestly service. But this chapter unfurls the beginning of a different kind of commission, as he is called to a prophetic career that takes place far away from his homeland. About a decade before the demolition of the temple where he was supposed to serve, this vision changes his life. Some interpreters note that Ezekiel is the most challenging prophetic book to interpret, and this expansive vision with winged beings having four different faces and *wheels within wheels* illustrates why. At the gates of Eden the tree of life is protected by cherubim in Genesis 3, while in the tabernacle there are winged cherubim protecting the ark of the covenant in Exodus 25, images that are presupposed and enhanced here in this distant land:

> *The form of the living beings had an appearance like blazing coals of fire, like the appearance of torches going back and forth between the living beings. The fire was bright, and lightning was flashing from the fire.* (Ezekiel 1:13)

This vision of the divine chariot that represents God's sovereign mobility and the sapphire throne that underscores God's transcendence is the prelude for Ezekiel's call to the prophetic office, much like Isaiah and Jeremiah before him. Often called the *son of Adam* or *mortal*, Ezekiel is commissioned to speak to the house of Israel in chapters 2–3, and when he eats a scroll that is offered to him it symbolizes that God's message to this rebellious people has been internalized. A sequence of prophetic signs and oracles in chapters 4–7 emphasize the urgency of the message. In the first of these signs, Ezekiel builds a clay model of the city of Jerusalem under siege (4:1–4), and along with the other signs of hair and food, dramatically illustrates the impending doom of the city and the reality that others will soon join them in exile.

Just over a year later, Ezekiel has another powerful experience. Whether he is teleported like Elijah (see 1 Kings 18) or enters into a trance, in chapters 8–11 Ezekiel is taken on a visionary excursion to the Jerusalem temple. It is here that he witnesses a shocking degree of corruption by seventy leaders, and even members of otherwise faithful and high-ranking families are complicit: we recall that the Shaphan family were supporters of Jeremiah, but in 8:10–13 he sees Jaazaniah along with some other figures engaging in forbidden rituals (compare the actions of Korah in Numbers 16). Not only is an execution order given in chapter 9, but the dazzling chariot departs in chapter 10, anticipating the coming destruction of the temple and the city. Nonetheless, in the aftermath of ruin and exile, there are divine words that provide glimmers of hope for a regathered people to dwell in a purified land:

> *I will give them one heart, and I will put a new spirit within them. I'll turn away their heart of stone and give them a heart of flesh, so that they will walk in my statutes, and keep and enact my judgments. They will be my people, and I will be their God.* (Ezekiel 11:19–20)

But days of restoration are a long way off. Meanwhile, in chapter 12 Ezekiel is instructed to pack a suitcase, part of a multilayered prophetic sign about the panic that accompanies invasion and exile (cf. Zedekiah's attempted escape in 2 Kings 25:4–5). The community needs to see this sign, because other "prophetic" voices in their midst are much more positive, and even using magical devices. Jeremiah also faced considerable opposition from other prophets who were declaring a quick end to Jerusalem's woes, and enjoyed popular support for their optimistic message. But in chapter 13 such misleading visions are roundly condemned by Ezekiel, followed up in chapter 14 with an indictment of the leaders who harbor secret idolatry in their hearts and have miserably lost the plot.

More than any other prophet so far, Ezekiel uses allegories and parables as part of his prophetic repertoire. Isaiah was told that God's people have been rebellious and hard of hearing, and now years later Ezekiel attempts to penetrate such defenses with elaborate analogies. For example, in chapter 15 Jerusalem is compared to the *wood of a grapevine*, not really useful for anything except burning. Furthermore, there is a longer allegory with graphic and disturbing images of unfaithfulness in chapter 16, taken to an even more extreme level in chapter 23. Other allegories include a tale of two eagles in chapter 17, and a princely lament in chapter 19 for the end of the Davidic monarchy with the captivity of Jehoiachin:

> *With hooks he was put in a cage, and they delivered him to the king of Babylon: they brought him into the stronghold so that his voice would no longer be heard on the mountains of Israel.* (Ezekiel 19:9)

At the halfway point of the book, chapter 24 begins on the day that Nebuchadnezzar lays siege to Jerusalem. Yet another allegory—this time of a cooking pot—opens the chapter, and is then followed by the most somber of prophetic signs: Ezekiel's wife dies, but he is told *not to mourn*, and the death of the prophet's wife becomes a depressing way of understanding the death of God's covenant partner. Finally, Ezekiel is told that on the day Israel's place of security is torn down, a fugitive will bring him the news, and at that moment his mouth will again be opened to speak.

Hour 30: Ezekiel 25–48

FOLLOWING THE ANNOUNCEMENT OF Nebuchadnezzar's siege of Jerusalem in Ezekiel 24, there is a long sequence of oracles against seven foreign nations in chapters 25–32. Such oracles are also part of the books of Isaiah and Jeremiah, and here in Ezekiel they serve a similar theological purpose: to illustrate the range of divine sovereignty in every sphere, and to declare that every nation is accountable for its actions. Chapter 25 addresses Israel's immediate neighbors around the compass points—Ammon, Moab, Edom, and Philistia—before turning to a longer oracle against Tyre and its king in chapters 26–28. Tyre ("rock") is a powerful island kingdom on the eastern Mediterranean coast with immense wealth from a vast trading network, but it will experience a titanic shipwreck along with its king (who is compared to a guardian cherub in Eden). After short message for the Sidonians, chapters 29–32 have a long oracle against Egypt and Pharaoh. This superpower, like Tyre, should expect a calamitous fall, and the Egyptian king is singled out with an ensnaring lament:

> *As a lion king of the nations you compare yourself, but you are like a monster of the sea. You burst forth in your rivers, muddy the waters with your feet, and foul the rivers. Thus says the Lord God: I will cast my net over you in the company of many peoples, and they will lift you out with my net.* (Ezekiel 32:2–3)

Back in chapter 24 it was announced that a fugitive would arrive with news of Jerusalem's collapse, and on that day Ezekiel's mouth would be opened. The night before the fugitive arrives in 33:21 to reveal "the city has fallen," the divine hand is upon the prophet and he is no longer speechless. Despite the worst report possible—that indeed Jerusalem has been destroyed—breathtaking oracles of restoration are then spoken in the next section of the book. For example, a prophetic word is announced in chapter

34 against the wayward "shepherds" of the nation who did not care for the needs of the flock, but God plans to rescue the lost sheep and appoint a Davidic shepherd to lead them with justice. Probably the most famous vision takes place in a valley full of dry bones in chapter 37. Ezekiel sees a picture of arid lifelessness of the ruined nation in exile, but in response to the prophetic word, the dry bones covering the floor of the valley are clothed with flesh and come to life in a corporate resurrection. The vision represents the divine promise of return to the land, for even though at this moment the house of Israel believe they are ill-fated and beyond hope, this prophetic word unveils a re-creation in the days ahead, *when I open your graves and bring you up from your graves, O my people, and when I put my spirit within you and rest you in your own land, then you will know that I, the Lord, have spoken and I have acted, declares the Lord* (Ezekiel 37:13–14).

Among the great mysteries in the book of Ezekiel is the identity of Gog from the land of Magog in chapters 38–39. Tubal, Meshech, and the land of Magog sound like they might be real places, but they have not yet been precisely identified with any certainty. Gog is characterized as the leader of an invading army from the far north who launches an assault on the restored people of Israel at some point *in the distant future*. Unknowingly, however, Gog is actually lured into this battle, where he and his hordes are soundly defeated, illustrating the kind of divine protection that the land can experience after the trials of exile. Whatever the origins of Gog, these images are used later in Revelation 20:8 in a climactic battle where divine power is manifested in a final victory against the forces of evil.

The centerpiece of the restoration to the land in the book of Ezekiel is the vision of the new temple in chapters 40–48. Assuming that his inaugural vision of the divine chariot in chapter 1 occurs when he is thirty years old, this closing vision in chapter 40 takes place two decades later when he is fifty, and customarily would be ready to retire from priestly service (Numbers 4:3). In this vision he is transported to a very high mountain and met by a shining bronze figure with measuring instruments in hand. In chapter 8, a similar guide led Ezekiel through the Jerusalem temple to witness the corruption, but here the prophet is conducted on a tour of the new temple complex to witness its dimensions and ornate details. Over the next few chapters Ezekiel sees the temple design with its gates and pillars, many rooms and courtyards, adorned with palm trees. Surely a high point of this vision is the return of the transcendent glory that had departed previously in chapter 10:

> *Then he led me to the gate, the gate that was facing the eastern way, and behold, the glory of the God of Israel come from the way of the east! His voice was like the sound of many waters, and the earth was shining because of his glory. The appearance of the vision was like the one I saw when he came to destroy the city, and just like the vision I saw by the Kebar river. I fell face down. Then the glory of the Lord entered the house by way of the eastern facing gate, and the spirit lifted me up and brought me to the inner courtyard, and behold, the Lord's glory filled the house.* (Ezekiel 43:1–5)

Through the eastern gate of the (old) temple, God's glory left (10:19) and the city was razed to the ground along with the house of the Lord. But now, Ezekiel glimpses a vision of the glory returning to the new temple, and this particular vision emphasizes the theme of divine presence that infuses the closing sections of the book. On the operational side, the next chapters outline the altar with its sacrifices and offerings, celebration of feasts, and sacred personnel from the Zadok line of the Levites. The allocation of lands suggests an equality among the tribes, with a *sacred area* at the center. Several times in this closing vision *the prince* is mentioned (cf. 37:25), and this character seems to be an ideal leader who serves alongside those worshipping in the temple, and presumably is a descendant of David.

Near the end of the vision Ezekiel sees water flowing from beneath the threshold of the temple, that incrementally turns into a river, leaving freshwater and teeming fish in its wake (47:1–12). The trees that line the river unfailingly bring forth fruit, and their leaves are for healing, inviting the reader to imagine this scene as a picture of the transformation brought by the gift of divine grace. Coupled with the name of the city in the final line—*The Lord is There*—this vision stresses the divine presence that overflows from the temple precincts into the entire land and completes the portrait of restoration in the second half of the book.

Hour 31: Hosea, Joel, Amos

After the three major prophets (Isaiah, Jeremiah, and Ezekiel), the next collection is often referred to as the "minor prophets." The term *minor* does not mean they are unimportant, but rather smaller in size compared to the long scrolls of the major prophets. However, ancient tradition referred to this collection as "the Book of the Twelve," and despite the various origins and historical contexts of each volume, they have been organized together as a group (and as it stands, roughly the same size as a major scroll). Assembled in roughly chronological order, some interwoven threads can be traced throughout the Book of the Twelve, such as a call to repent, the *day of the Lord*, and prospects for hope after disaster. As a prophetic anthology, these voices provide a chorus of perspectives on the character of God and the identity of God's people.

Opening the collection is the book of Hosea, located in the time period prior to the Assyrian demolition of the north. While he is a contemporary of Isaiah, Hosea is from the north, and is active during the reign of Jeroboam II (see 2 Kings 14:23–29), a period of economic prosperity and spiritual poverty. Family members of the prophets have been used as signs before: Isaiah's kids are given symbolic names that forecast the exile, Jeremiah is told be single because God has no spouse, and Ezekiel cannot mourn the death of his wife. Hosea's marriage to Gomer is also used as a sign, and Gomer's unfaithfulness is an image of how the people abandon God for other forms of satisfaction. The names of Hosea's children in chapter 1 illustrate how God will nonetheless extend compassion to these wayward people, further underscored in chapter 3 when Hosea has to buy Gomer back from slavery:

> *I said to her, "For many days you will live with me, and not be promiscuous, and I will be yours." To be sure, for many days the children*

> *of Israel will live without king or prince, without sacrifice or sacred pillars, without ephod or idols. But afterwards the children of Israel will return and seek the Lord their God and David their king, and they will tremble before the Lord and his goodness in the last days.* (Hosea 3:3–5)

The divine longings refracted through Hosea's familial experiences form a segue to the medley of poetic oracles in chapters 4–14 that both build on this marriage imagery and branch off in new directions. For instance, in chapter 5 the prophet denounces northern Israel by telling them that their lecherous impulses prevent them from returning to God, while the beginning of chapter 6 features a prophetic voice that urges the people to pursue obedience that will result in a refreshing experience of God like *spring rains that water the earth* (6:3). In chapter 9 the citizens are told to expect to eat unclean food in Assyria as a consequence of turning away from God (enhanced in 13:11, *I gave you a king in my anger, and took him away in my wrath*), but the book closes in chapter 14 with images of that same God generously receiving them back in love, so they can blossom in the vineyard of their inheritance.

Next up in the Book of the Twelve is Joel, but unlike Hosea, there is no superscription that locates the book in any particular reign or era. A surplus of priestly images suggests that Joel is located in the south, but there are no biographical details about Joel himself. Instead, the book begins abruptly with a frightening description of a swarming plague of locusts, leaving nothing in their path as they choke the land. The images of ecological infestation, using four different Hebrew words for locusts in 1:4, is then applied to an invading army that sweeps in and overruns everything. If the land is like Eden before, it is only a burned wasteland after this army comes through, and nothing can escape (2:3). The response to this "day" of gloomy darkness and sense of utter helplessness is a call to acts of repentance, as the prophet issues a plea for the people to recalibrate their lives with fasting and sorrow for sin (2:12). But judgment is not the final word, for in the wake of such devastation there is also a divine assurance:

> *I will compensate you for the years that the swarming locust has eaten . . . After this, I will pour out my spirit upon all flesh: your sons and daughters will prophesy, your old men will dream dreams and your young men will see visions.* (Joel 2:25, 28)

In the New Testament book of Acts this outpouring of the spirit plays a key role in a game-changing speech by the apostle Peter (Acts 2:17–21).

Here in the book of Joel, this spiritual renaissance is part of an era of restoration, as the citizens now dwell in a land where vats overflow and threshing floors are piled with grain. With some ironic retribution, those nations that desolated Judah will themselves be made desolate and judged for their atrocities. The concluding movements of the book indicate that Jerusalem will enjoy an ideal future, as the hills drip with milk and arid places of Judah flow with fresh water.

Amos is a contemporary of Hosea, and according to the book's superscription, lives in the time period when Uzziah reigns in the south and Jeroboam II in the north. There is an ominous notice that Amos is active *two years before the earthquake*, and whatever else this means (cf. Zech 14:5), it is an overture to the thundering oracles of judgment that are about to be declared in this book. Amos's name means *burden*, and we discover that he is a shepherd from the south who ventures into the northern kingdom to call out its abusive behavior and violations of the covenant. Amos is from the village of Tekoa in Judah, the home of an actress who previously appeared in 2 Samuel 14. Indeed, this prophetic book begins with some serious acting, as Amos is dressed in mourning garments and arrives in the north chanting a funeral lament. The crowd must be excited that Amos is pronouncing death to Israel's enemies—such as Damascus, Tyre, Moab, and even southern Judah—but then he turns the tables in chapter 2 to denounce northern Israel itself and proclaim its imminent demise. The funeral oration becomes an introduction to the intense oracles that follow, as Amos castigates the northerners for economic inequality and related injustices as they consume alcohol by the bowlful but do not grieve for their awful state:

> *Therefore, because you trample the poor with taxes and demand burdens of grain from them, you will not live in your finely crafted houses, and will not drink the wine from your choice vineyards.* (Amos 5:11)

These oracles of condemnation raise the ire of the religious leaders in Bethel, and in 7:10–17 there is a confrontation with Amaziah, the priest of Bethel. Amos is ordered to go back to Judah and earn a prophetic livelihood there, but he responds to Amaziah with the account of his divine calling—that has echoes of Moses's call from the flock in Exodus 3—and proceeds to carry on with his pronouncements of judgment. The book begins with reference to an *earthquake*, and in 9:9 there is a declaration that the house of Israel will soon be *shaken*. Yet for all of the fierce denunciations, the final lines of the book (9:11–15) end on a more upbeat note of restoration down the road: the *fallen tent of David* will be repaired, along with the rebuilding of ruined cities and the prospects of an abundant harvest as evidence of God's beneficence.

Hour 32: Obadiah, Jonah, Micah

The shortest book of the Twelve, and of the entire Hebrew Bible, is Obadiah. Little is known about this figure—his name means *servant of the Lord*—but the 291 words of the book mainly recount an event presumably at the time of the Babylonian demolition of Jerusalem, and involve the neighboring Edomites. There is a long-standing rivalry between Israel and Edom, beginning with the brothers Jacob and Esau, and continuing through the days of the monarchy and beyond. The particular grievance in Obadiah involves how the Edomites took advantage of the foreign attack for their own gain, and gleefully joined the looting in the destroyed city after the lengthy siege:

> *On that day you stood off in the distance, on the day when strangers carried off its wealth. When foreigners entered its gate and cast lots for Jerusalem, even you were just like one of them.* (Obadiah 11).

A strong current of revenge flows through this oracle, and as already seen in prophetic literature, nations are accountable for their actions. Edom is no exception, and just as they plundered their neighbor, so they themselves will be plundered by those whom they thought were allies. At the end of this short book, the Edomite threat is vanquished and the people dwell securely in their land. Thus, the Edomites seem to represent all hostile threats that eventually will be nullified by God. Nonetheless, perhaps Obadiah includes an implicit caution about any gloating by the people of God, a topic that is also explored in Proverbs 24:17–18.

Surely the most famous of the Book of the Twelve is Jonah, whose remarkable voyage has been referenced in both great works of art and an episode of *The Simpsons*. Jonah son of Amittai himself has a brief cameo in 2 Kings 14, where he is active in the northern kingdom during the reign of Jeroboam II, preaching about expanding the borders of Israel in the dangerous days of the Assyrian empire. The book of Jonah begins with the prophet's call to proclaim a message of judgment against Nineveh, the capital city of Assyria. But instead of responding in obedience, Jonah flees in the opposite direction and sails toward Tarshish and the ends of the earth. God appoints a storm so severe that the very ship itself fears it will break apart (1:4), and with increasing desperation, the sailors discover that Jonah is the reason for the storm and reluctantly agree to throw him overboard. However, God appoints a large fish to swallow the resistant prophet, and over the course of three days and three nights in the creature's belly, Jonah's prayer closes on the following note:

> *"With a voice of thanksgiving I will sacrifice to you, what I have vowed I will repay, salvation belongs to the Lord." Then the Lord spoke to the fish, and it vomited Jonah onto the dry ground.* (Jonah 2:9–10)

For a second time the divine word comes to Jonah, but on this occasion he does travel to Nineveh, and delivers a very short and vague oracle of judgment. Startlingly, the citizens respond with belief, and there is citywide repentance. The standard position in prophetic literature is that Assyria is a cruel and rapacious empire, so this contrite posture in the capital city is completely unexpected. Even the king is dressed in sackcloth as a sign of mourning, and everyone—including the cattle—is commanded to cry out urgently to God (3:7–9). Upon seeing their repentance, God chooses to not send calamity. Altogether, this turn of events makes Jonah one of the most "successful" prophets ever, but his reaction is decidedly negative. Evidently Jonah would prefer that the citizens of Nineveh be destroyed, and complains about divine compassion as he sits on the edge of the city (4:5). By ending with some dialogue and a question from God, the book concludes on a note of challenge to Jonah (and the reader) about the extraordinary horizons of grace, and divine willingness to extend mercy to the undeserving.

Micah is located at the halfway juncture of the Book of the Twelve, and this prophet was active during the reigns of the southern kings Jotham, Ahaz, and Hezekiah, when the northern city of Samaria was destroyed. In 2 Kings 16 a litany of corruptions in the Ahaz regime are noted, and Micah's oracles that expose flawed leadership and spiritual abuses stem from this period. Overlapping with the career of Isaiah—who was probably slightly older—Micah has some shared themes with Isaiah, and denounces similar kinds of social inequities. In terms of structure, the book interweaves words of judgment with promises of salvation, and while forecasting the demise of Jerusalem, also envisions its renewal afterwards:

> *Be in pain and scream, Daughter Zion, like a woman in labor. For you now are about to go out of the city and dwell in the fields, and you will go to Babylon. There you will be rescued, there the Lord will redeem you from the grasp of your enemies.* (Micah 4:10)

Moresheth, the hometown of Micah, is a village twenty miles or so from Jerusalem. Given Micah's rural background, he has a different perspective on urban decadence and spiritual decay. But there is another village at the center of attention in chapter 5, the town of Bethlehem. The birthplace of David, it is predicted that in the future a ruler will emerge from this village who will shepherd the people of Israel (5:1). Along with this reference to Bethlehem, the other most quoted section of Micah is a beautiful and strident critique of deviant temple practices. King Ahaz imports all sorts of Assyrian beliefs into the temple in order to appease the superpower (see 2 Kings 16:10–18), so perhaps Micah is presenting a countermove in chapter 6. His words are not a rejection of sacrifices, as such, but rather a reminder of the essential vision of relational connection with God:

> *What should I bring in order to meet with God, and bow down before God on high? Should I enter his presence with burnt offerings and year-old calves? Is the Lord pleased with thousands of rams or ten thousand rivers of oil? Should I give my firstborn for my transgressions, the fruit of my body for the sin of my soul? He has already told you, O human being, what is good and what the Lord seeks from you: to do justice, love faithfulness, and in humility to walk with your God.* (Micah 6:6–8)

It should be noted that in the book of Jeremiah—as we recall, situated in the days of the Babylonian invasion—the prophetic words of Micah are actually quoted as a cautionary tale. At a pivotal moment, Jeremiah is arrested and nearly sentenced to death by the leading officials (Jer 26:16–19). However, some of the elders intervene by citing an oracle of Micah from Moresheth about Zion being plowed like a field and Jerusalem turned into a pile of rubble (3:12). The elders use this example as a challenge to take seriously the prophetic word, and by extension it is an impetus for later readers to likewise respond.

Hour 33: Nahum, Habakkuk, Zephaniah

Like Jonah, the city of Nineveh is a central spatial setting in the book of Nahum. But Jonah's prophetic utterance is only five words in Hebrew, whereas Nahum features three complex chapters and a multilayered oracle against the capital city of Assyria. Uniquely among the Twelve, Nahum's vision about Nineveh is referred to as a *book* in the superscription. But otherwise, not much is known about the prophet. He is from the village of Elkosh, which must be small because this the only place in the Bible it is mentioned. Scholars mention an irony: here is an Israelite from an obscure village proclaiming the downfall of this mighty superpower. It might therefore be assumed that Nahum's book addresses a situation approximately a century after Jonah, when Nineveh is at the pinnacle of power. Starting with a portrait of God as a divine warrior who dries up rivers and pours out anger like fire, the Assyrians are informed that they are dealing with a more formidable opponent than they have ever faced:

> *Whatever you are devising against the Lord, he will totally destroy.*
> *No adversary rises up against him twice!* (Nahum 1:9)

An extended sequence that depicts a city under siege forms the core of chapter 2, with a flurry of snapshots of an invading army that assaults and plunders the previously secure capital. Chapter 3 then presents Nineveh as a victim ravaged by an oppressor, as retribution for previous crimes and aggressions. Perhaps the violent and horrid images in chapter 3 are intended to portray Nineveh not just in historical terms, but also as a representative for any tyrannical and rapacious regime that vaunts itself and inflicts malice on others. If so, then it is notable that *Nahum* is a name that means *comfort*, and thus the book might be designed to illustrate that all such regimes will eventually be called to account for their actions. The assurance of such justice might well be a comfort to all who have suffered at the hands of such brutality.

Habakkuk's first words (*How long will I cry for help, O Lord, and you do not hear? I cry out "Violence," but you do not save!*) set the stage for a dialogue between the prophet and God. Few details are given about Habakkuk, but it would appear that he is active between the Assyrian demolition of the north and prior to the Babylonian assault on the south. As in the psalms of lament, the prophet complains to God about rampant injustice in a vicious world (1:2–4), but the divine response can hardly be reassuring, as God outlines the forthcoming movement of Babylonian troops. As a result, a central question in the book is how God can use a nation as horrible as Babylon—even given the guilt and folly of Judah—as an instrument of discipline. In another divine response in chapter 2, there is a challenge that *the righteous will live by faith* even while injustice is rampant and God's punishment is withheld, a pivotal sentence in the apostle Paul's New Testament Letter to the Romans. A series of "woe" oracles underline the certainty of God's justice in due course:

> *Woe to whoever builds a city with bloodshed, or establishes a town with wickedness. Behold, is it not from the Lord of hosts that the people's labor will burn, and the nations weary themselves for nothing? For the earth will be filled with the knowledge of the Lord's glory, just as the waters cover the sea.* (Habakkuk 2:12–14)

The wrestling of Habakkuk moves to a climax in chapter 3. The superscription at the beginning of the chapter and the postscript at the end suggest that this chapter is a kind of hymn that would be performed in the temple. If so, it functions here as a testimony, with the prophet resolving to hold fast to the promises of God even in the vicissitudes of life. By way of structure, the book opens with a litany of complaints, but concludes on a note of determined trust: although the fig tree does not blossom and there is no herd in the stalls, says the prophet, *I will yet rejoice in the Lord, and have joy in the God of my salvation* (3:17–18). As for his name, some scholars argue that Habakkuk is related to the Hebrew verb *embrace*, as seen in 2 Kings 4:16, when the prophet Elisha tells the childless Shunammite woman that she will *embrace* a son. Given the travail and suffering in that episode—but also the ultimate consolation when she embraces her son who has been raised from the dead when the prophet Elisha intercedes—the idea of "embrace" is a compelling suggestion for Habakkuk's name.

Zephaniah is active during the reign of King Josiah in Judah, and may have the most interesting genealogy in the Book of the Twelve: *Cushi* is usually a reference to someone with Ethiopian descent, and some interpreters posit that *Hezekiah* is the earlier king. If so, Zephaniah speaks as an insider with royal blood and an aristocratic heritage. Since Jeremiah's early days also take place in the reign of Josiah, we can assume that these two prophets overlap during the very stressful buildup to the Babylonian assault. Josiah's leadership is comparatively positive (his grandfather Manasseh is considered the worst king), and includes some movement toward national renewal. But Zephaniah's opening phrase (*I will utterly sweep away everything from the face of the earth, declares the Lord*) indicates a more deeply ingrained malaise. Josiah's reforms include dismantling Baal altars (2 Kings 23:4), but the effects of such installations lingered long after any architecture was removed. Chapter 1 features an oracle spoken against the land of Judah, and an announcement of the day of the Lord that will be accompanied by gloom and the densest clouds (1:15), and no amount of silver or gold can help anyone on that day (1:18). Chapter 2 starts with a call to repentance, before unfolding a series of oracles against foreign nations such as Philistia, Moab, and Assyria. However, corruption and subsequent judgment are not the last word in the book, as chapter 3 presents words of hope and promise after calamity. God will search through Jerusalem with lamps in order to punish those who are wickedly apathetic (1:12), but that same city of Jerusalem will also be soothed and consoled:

> *On that day it will be said to Jerusalem, "Don't be afraid, O Zion, don't let your hands fall slack. The Lord your God is in your midst, a warrior mighty to save. He will rejoice over you with joy, he will quiet you with his love, rejoicing over you with songs of joy."* (Zephaniah 3:16–17)

Hour 34: Haggai, Zechariah, Malachi

THE LAST THREE BOOKS of the Twelve all take place in the postexilic period, and while the people of God have returned to the land, there are lots of political and economic problems as they live in the shadow of the empire. The book of Haggai begins with a specific chronology: in the second year of the Persian emperor Darius I, the divine word of the Lord is communicated through the hand of Haggai ("festival"), who is also mentioned in the book of Ezra. Haggai's word is directed to a pair of leaders in this struggling community, Zerubbabel ("sown in Babylon") the governor and Joshua the high priest. Despite the people's inclination that the present moment is *not* the right time to (re)build the temple, Haggai's word challenges them to look at their dismal circumstances and reconsider their priorities (1:2–11). So far, we have mainly seen the prophets ignored (or worse), but Haggai is taken seriously, and within a few weeks they set to work. Admittedly, the early progress is not very impressive, but in chapter 2 there is an indication that the best is yet to come:

> *For thus says the Lord of hosts, "In just a little while I again will shake the heavens and the earth, the sea and the dry ground. And I will shake all the nations, and they will come with the wealth of nations and I will fill this house with glory," says the Lord of hosts.* (Haggai 2:6–7)

Despite the meager beginnings of the restoration project, Haggai assures the community that the glory of the new house will eclipse the glory of the former one, and peace will be granted in this place (2:9). The book closes with a summons to remember this particular moment and compare the blessings that follow, in addition to a final word about Zerubbabel being under the umbrella of divine protection even as God overthrows kingdoms and overturns chariots along with their drivers (2:21–23), carrying echoes of the exodus event.

The longest and probably the most bewildering book of the Twelve is Zechariah. Like Haggai, Zechariah's prophetic work is mentioned in Ezra, and thus he is active during the same period in the postexilic community. But unlike Haggai's relatively straightforward exhortation to prioritize the house of God over one's personal house, Zechariah is brimming with arresting visions and highly imaginative utterances. The book begins, though, with a very clear call to the people: they have returned to the land, but now they need to fully return to God (1:2–6), and the community responds with an acknowledgment of their past failures. After this introduction, there is an eightfold sequence of *night visions*. These visions are designed to help Zechariah's community return to a wholehearted confidence in God's reality for their lives. So, in 1:7–17 Zechariah sees a rider on a red horse, and shortly discovers four horses—representing the four points of the compass—that form a divine patrol, keeping track of activities on the earth:

> *They answered the angel of the Lord who was standing between the myrtle trees, and said, "We've walked around the earth, and behold, all the earth sits still and quiet." The angel of the Lord answered, "O Lord of hosts, for how long will you not show compassion to Jerusalem and the cities of Judah, who you have been angry with these seventy years?" Then the Lord answered the angel, the one speaking with me, with good and comforting words.* (Zechariah 1:11–13)

Occurring on a single night, the eight visions in chapters 1–6 also include: blacksmiths striking the horns that scattered Judah (1:18–21), a surveyor who can no longer measure Jerusalem because of its vast population (2:1–5), a cleansing of the high priest who is accused by Satan (3:1–10), two olive trees giving oil for a golden lampstand that illuminates the world (4:1–14), a flying scroll (5:1–4), a woman in a container (5:5–11), and four chariots moving out to accomplish the divine purpose (6:1–8). An intriguing character is "the Branch," evidently a royal figure who will arise in the days ahead (3:8; 6:12). Together these visions and utterances represent an encouragement to not only finish the temple project, but also to live out its theology. This is probably why chapters 7–8 pause to reflect on a debate about fasting, as some people wonder if they should continue to commemorate the temple's earlier destruction. In response, Zechariah outlines some present-tense ethical imperatives (e.g., administer true justice, and in your hearts do not think evil of one another) in anticipation of an unprecedented future:

> *Thus says the Lord of hosts: it will yet be that peoples will arrive, even the citizens of many cities, and each will go to the other saying, "Let's go at once to ask for the favor of the Lord and seek the Lord of hosts, I'm going myself!" So, many peoples and mighty nations will arrive to seek the Lord of hosts in Jerusalem, and to ask for the Lord's favor.* (Zechariah 8:20–22)

Zechariah concludes with a sequence of complex oracles in chapters 9–14, ranging from divine initiative against foreign nations and the people's restoration in the land, to images of transformation and the comprehensiveness of God's rule. Of interest to New Testament writers is Zechariah's picture of a messianic king riding on a humble donkey rather than a warhorse that intimidates a kingdom through violence, a prophetic word that features in the passion narratives of the Gospels (9:9–10; cf. Matt 21:5, John 12:15). By all accounts Zechariah is part of a priestly family (Iddo is mentioned in Nehemiah 12), and his passion for the temple and God's presence is manifest from start to finish.

Malachi is the final book of the Twelve, and takes place some years later than Haggai and Zechariah, after the temple has been rebuilt. His name means *my messenger*, but it might function as a title rather than a proper name since it nowhere else occurs in the Bible. The book's approach is to take questions that people are struggling with or "words on the street" and turn them into oracles, a style that is referred to as *prophetic disputation*. Whether many are discouraged by their circumstance or stressed out by life in the empire's shadow, they are only half-heartedly entering into worship at the temple. Such a situation is indicated in the low quality of their offerings (1:8), which surely the political governor would not receive with favor. Later in the book such actions are referred to as robbing God (3:8), and the people are challenged to prioritize God in every area and then measure their lives accordingly. Various questions are addressed in the book, and perhaps most poignant is the complaint that *it is futile to serve God* (3:14), especially when evildoers apparently prosper. Malachi closes the Book of the Twelve—and indeed, it is the last book of the Christian Bible, and precedes Matthew in the New Testament—and draws to a conclusion by rehearsing the day of the Lord that is coming, when an Elijah-figure should be expected to usher in a new era:

Hour 34: Haggai, Zechariah, Malachi

Remember the law of Moses my servant that I commanded him at Horeb, the statutes and judgements for all Israel. Behold, I will send you Elijah the prophet before the great and dreadful day of the Lord comes. He will return the hearts of the fathers to the children and the hearts of the children to their fathers, lest I come and strike the land with destruction. (Malachi 4:4–5)

Hour 35: Psalms 1–72

THE COLLECTION OF 150 psalms (*songs with instruments*) can be listened to as a soundtrack to the faith of Israel. This anthology of greatest hits is organized in five "books" that follow the broad contours of Israel's history: beginning with the early and turbulent days of the monarchy, through the dismal collapse and exile, and into the restoration period with a glance at the horizons beyond. It is likely that these songs were originally intended for public performance, and provided a faith perspective even in the midst of the stresses and strains of everyday life, with a variety of genres such as thanksgiving, lament, petition, praise, and historical psalms.

Book 1 (Psalms 1–41) begins with a pair of compositions that function as an overture to the entire collection. The first psalm outlines two contrasting *pathways* in life: the way of reflecting on God's word leads to stability, whereas the path of the wicked is unstable and quite literally vanishes in the end. In Psalm 2 the notion of competing kingships is unveiled, and although the nations may plot against God's anointed king, they will never completely succeed (quite boldly this poem presents God as *laughing* at such futile efforts). Psalm 3 immediately attracts attention because of its superscription: *a psalm of David.* These titles are probably part of the temple liturgy, and among other things, indicate the genre of the psalm. In this case, Psalm 3 is a Davidic composition, suggesting that it tells a story of royal struggle and divine care, e.g., *many are my foes . . . but you O Lord are a shield around me* (3:1–3). The next sequence, Psalms 4–22, includes a number of topics, but crisis is a common thread. At the halfway point of Book 1 is arguably the most famous composition, Psalm 23, which begins with the image of God as a shepherd and continues through a harrowing journey:

Even though I walk through the valley of death's shadow,

I do not fear evil, because you are with me.
Your scepter and your staff, they give me courage.
You arrange a table before me in the presence of my adversaries,
You soothe my head with oil, my cup flows over. (Psalm 23:4–5)

Psalm 23 concludes with a vivid description of divine faithfulness (the powerful Hebrew term *hesed* is seen earlier in a texts such as Exodus 15:13 and Deuteronomy 5:10) relentlessly *pursuing* after the poet over the course of an entire lifetime. In many ways the Psalms is a very personal book, and even when conveying matters of national import and geopolitical chaos, it still speaks to the heart with striking metaphors and memorable imagery. The second half of Book 1 continues the theme of lament, and also includes reflections on the temple (*who can ascend to the mountain of the Lord, who can dwell in his holy place?*, 24:3), compositions about wisdom (*I will instruct and teach you in the way you should go*, 32:8), and concludes with Psalm 41, where God is portrayed as the helper of someone in great need.

Book 2 (Psalms 42–72) begins with a poet longing for the house of God (*as the deer pants after streams of water*), with hints of various disasters and the coming exile where the entire community is dislocated from the living water of the temple. Psalm 42 is a *Korah* composition, with echoes of the infamous rebellion in Numbers 16 where the descendants of Korah survive and become musicians of theology. Books 1 and 2 do not follow a strict chronological ordering, but rather provide a series of snapshots of faith and life in the age of the monarchy, with all its tumult but also with an awareness of God's faithfulness throughout. In general, many psalms in Book 2 trace numerous fears and anxieties as the various invasions of Assyria and Babylon draw near, but also look toward the reliability of divine promise amidst such heartbreak. Notable in Book 2 are a number of other superscriptions that reference various events in the life of King David. One example is Psalm 51, with an ambiance that reflects the sordid affair with Bathsheba and the confrontation of Nathan the prophet. The poet of this psalm confesses and asks for mercy:

Create in me a clean heart, O God,
a right spirit make new within me.
Do not cast me from your presence,
or take your holy spirit away from me.
Return to me the joy of your salvation,
and sustain me with a wholehearted spirit. (Psalm 51:10–12)

Psalm 51 ends with an affirmation that the sacrifice of God is a broken spirit, and a request that God rebuild the walls of Jerusalem. Other psalms in Book 2 variously characterize the royal enemies as a pack of dogs howling throughout the night (Psalm 59), or a longing to be under the provisions of divine care (*lead me to the rock that is higher than I*, 61:2). Furthermore, the lengthy Psalm 68 has many stanzas that are difficult to interpret, but draws on ancient images of God's power in the past (e.g., when God marched before the people in the wilderness, the earth heaved and even Mount Sinai was quaking, vv. 7–8) in order to nurture a vision of hope for the future (e.g., one day the kings of nations will arrive with gifts because of the Jerusalem temple, v. 29).

It should be clear by now that the book of Psalms is a work of poetry. We have already encountered extended stretches of biblical poetry in Isaiah and other great writing prophets, and there are shorter examples in Genesis to Kings as well. One feature of English poetry is the rhyming of sounds at the end of the line. Hebrew poetry, at its most basic level, is a "rhyming" of images or ideas, usually called *parallelism*, and there are a number of different varieties. As an example, consider Psalm 71 right near the end of Book 2. The speaker in this psalm certainly sounds aged and experienced, and even though rescue is desperately needed, remains willing to trust God's character. In the poetic lines cited below, we can notice the rhyming of images in the poet's testimony and willingness to not give up in the face of a deadly conspiracy:

> *My mouth is full of your praise,*
> *all day long with your glory.*
> *Do not throw me away at the time of old age,*
> *when my strength has finished, do not abandon me.*
> *For my enemies are speaking against me,*
> *Those watching for my life take counsel together.* (Psalm 71:8–10)

Hour 36: Psalms 73–150

Books 1 (1–41) and 2 (42–72) of the Psalms provide a window into the turbulent period of the monarchy in northern and southern Israel. Book 3 (73–89) is arguably the lowest point, as this collection reflects the trauma of the exile and its aftermath. A high percentage of lament psalms are found in Book 3, along with haunting descriptions of the temple's demolition and the isolation from the land of promise. The opening composition, Psalm 73, has the name *Asaph* in the superscription, and in Ezra 3:10 "the sons of Asaph" are a musical group. Psalm 73 starts with a confession that the poet's feet had almost stumbled, and the poet admits to feeling intense envy upon seeing the prosperity of the wicked. Back in Psalm 1 we recall that the way of the wicked eventually vanishes, but for this poet, those who have no regard for God seem healthy and materially successful. However, the turning point occurs when the poet enters the holy places of God (73:17), and receives renewed perspective on the instability and ultimate fate of the unfaithful.

The destruction of the Jerusalem temple is recounted with painful detail in Psalm 74, as the place where God meets with humanity is hacked apart by barbarians *wielding axes like they were striking a gnarled tree*, destroying all the *carved work* before burning the rest of the structure (74:5–7). There is a call for God to act and respond in Psalm 74, a plea that is often reiterated in the prayers that follow, as in the chastened questions of 79:5, *How long, O Lord? Will you be angry forever, will your jealous wrath keep burning?* But there are stirrings of hope along the way: in Psalm 82 there is a courtroom scene where the gods of the nations are on trial for neglecting the poor and sentenced to death, while in Psalm 84 there is a stirring desire to make the journey toward the house of the Lord when arid deserts are transformed into pools of water. Nonetheless, the bleakness of exile is captured in Psalm 88 as the poet wrestles with the silence and apparent abandonment of God:

> *For my soul is full of miseries, my life is touching Sheol.*
> *I am counted among those who descend to the Pit,*
> *I have become like a warrior whose strength is lost.*
> *Among the dead I drift, like those slain, lying in the grave,*
> *those you remember no more, cut off from your hand.*
> *In the lowest of pits you've put me,*
> *in the darkest of places, in the deepest of waters.* (Psalm 88:3–6)

Book 4 (90–106) unfolds a new beginning, the rebuilding of a broken world and a restoration in the aftermath of exile. The first composition, Psalm 90, carries a superscription that refers to Moses, and draws the congregation back to an earlier period, long before the advent of kings and kingdoms. Acknowledging that God has been their *dwelling place* all along, this psalm reorients the community to a reliance on divine promise and guidance rather than the seductions and coercion of the cultures around them. Notably, the grouping of Psalms 93–99 is referred to as the *enthronement songs*, encouraging the people to recognize that God is their monarch, with sovereignty that has no limits. Psalm 93 proclaims that God's throne is above (and therefore undisturbed by) the raging waters of chaos, and Psalm 99 reminds the community that God is seated amidst the powerful cherubim (cf. Exodus 25:17–22). Furthermore, Psalm 103 makes the provocative claim that God is not fair, that is, *he does not treat us as our sins deserve*: instead, as far as the east is from the west, so he has removed our transgressions far away from us.

The final composition of Book 4, Psalm 106, is a historical review with similarities to 105, but focusing on how the people of God went astray early and often. Rebellion occurs in *Egypt*, when the ancestors failed to perceive divine wonders and even rebelled at the *Red Sea*. The pattern continues in the *wilderness* with a lack of trust and cravings, in *the camp* with the jealousy of Moses's leadership, building the golden calf at Horeb, attaching themselves to the Baal of *Peor* and eating sacrifices offered to the dead, provoking wrath at the waters of *Meribah*, and offering child sacrifices in the land of *Canaan*. These seven geographical sites, with multiple instances of flagrant sin occurring in each, indicate the comprehensiveness of the rebellion over multiple generations. But the number seven also represents the completeness of divine forgiveness, and illustrates how symmetrically God distributes grace. On the one hand the people are scattered among the foreign nations as a consequence of their disobedience, but on the other hand, God responds in mercy to the prayer that functions as the poetic capstone:

Save us, O Lord our God,
and gather us from the nations,
in order to give thanks to your holy name,
to revel in your praise. (Psalm 106:47)

Book 5 (107–150) opens with an emphatic response to the closing prayer of Psalm 106. Indeed, the first lines of Psalm 107 are a resounding declaration of God's faithful love, with a lengthy report of regathering the scattered people from every point on the compass. Some themes of Book 5 include the celebration of return from exile, rebuilding the community that has been restored to the land, and looking ahead to new avenues of divine activity among the people of God. Psalm 111 starts with *hallelujah* ("praise the Lord"), the first of many occurrences of this imperative in Book 5. The collection of Psalms 113–118 is often called the Egyptian Passover collection and use the images of the original exodus in order to commemorate a second release as the community has been rescued from Babylonian captivity and brought through another kind of wilderness. Psalm 117 (later quoted in Romans 15:11) is the shortest composition in the entire book, and yet it contains a big irony, as the foreign nations themselves are called upon to give praise because of God's steadfast love to Israel:

Praise the Lord, all nations,
applaud him, all peoples!
For great is his faithfulness toward us,
and the truth of the Lord is everlasting,
Praise the Lord! (Psalm 117)

If Psalm 117 is the shortest, then breaking the record for the longest is Psalm 119, an alphabetic (or acrostic) composition that celebrates the central place of the Torah in the believer's life (e.g., v. 32, *I will run in the way of your commands, for you have expanded my heart*). After 119 is another collection, the *Songs of Ascents* (Psalms 120–134) that reboots the genre of pilgrimage hymns and applies them to a new generation who are making the festive journeys up to Jerusalem. The collection begins with the image of a worshipper longing to make the journey (120–121), and moves to a climax with an all-night celebration in the house of God (135). Closer to the end of Book 5, Psalm 137 captures the painful memories of the trauma of captivity (*By the rivers of Babylon, there we sat, there we wept when we remembered Zion*) with a frightening invective directed toward their captors (vv. 8–9), while the poet of Psalm 139 is in awe of God's intimate creative activity (e.g., v. 13, *you formed my inward parts, you wove me together in my mother's womb*).

The conclusion of Book 5, and of the Psalter as a whole, is the orchestral concert of Psalm 150. Every category of instrument (percussion, wind, string) combined with voices and dancing makes for a full-bodied expression of gratitude and acknowledgment. All the crisis, lament, and poetic responses to suffering and disappointment now move aside in this final psalm in order to create the music of unfettered praise. Psalm 1 declares that the way of the wicked will vanish, and here there is no obvious sign of evil at the end of the book of Psalms. Instead, the last composition, Psalm 150, operates as an open-ended and ongoing summons, as every living creature is invited to give praise for who God is, what God does, and the reality that God dwells in the divine palace, reigning without threat and enthroned above chaos.

> *Praise God in his sanctuary, praise him in the skies of his strength! Praise him for his powerful deeds, praise him for his unsurpassed greatness! . . . Let every living thing that has breath praise the Lord!* (Psalm 150:1–2, 6)

Hour 37: Proverbs

"Wisdom" has an expansive definition in the ancient world, ranging from technical skill (such as building or sailing) all the way to song writing and financial investments. Based on this definition, it is not surprising that wisdom was a sought-after commodity in the ancient Near East, with wisdom literature attested in many different cultures from Egypt to Mesopotamia. There have already been numerous examples of stories with wisdom (*hokhmah*) in biblical texts so far: early in Genesis 2–3 wisdom and knowledge are important themes, Joseph is acclaimed as wise by the Egyptian pharaoh (Gen 41:29), Joshua is filled with the spirit of wisdom as he prepares to take over leadership upon the death of Moses (Deuteronomy 34:9), and Solomon receives the gift of wisdom in 1 Kings: *God gave wisdom to Solomon, and great depth of discernment, and a breadth of mind like the sand on the shore of the sea* (4:29). The application of wisdom is more than just accumulating facts for their own sake, but rather exercising sound judgment and living well, learning to make prudent choices as the journey of life is navigated. Character formation, therefore, is a central purpose of wisdom literature, nurturing the capacity to make the best choices in the maelstrom of everyday life with its many experiences and daily dramas.

A number of biblical books are classified as wisdom literature, and one particular anthology of material is found in the book of Proverbs. The opening line—*The proverbs of Solomon, son of David, king of Israel, to know wisdom and instruction, to understand words of insight*—associates it with the name of the eminently wise king, and a common suggestion is that the court of Solomon initially began the process of collecting and organizing Israel's repository of wisdom. But a glance back at 1 Kings 1–11 reveals that Solomon himself—despite this immense gift—did not finish well, and is directly responsible for the division of the kingdom. Whether his name is used as a kind of cautionary tale is an open question. The book of Proverbs insists from the outset that the pursuit of wisdom needs to be predicated on *the fear of the Lord*. Numerous times this phrase occurs in the book, but it should not be construed as "scared" or "terrified." Rather, the fear of the Lord is a healthy respect, and an awareness that God ultimately has humanity's best interests in mind.

The book of Proverbs is organized in seven unequal parts—often marked with a superscription—starting with a long opening section in chapters 1 to 9. Usually proverbs (*mishlei*) are short sentences of two balanced or offsetting lines, but chapters 1 to 9 mainly feature longer compositions with various kinds of dramatic situations. In the first chapter, for example, there is an extended sequence in verses 8–19 with a warning against violence with a group of friends or associates, and the temptation to gather wealth through dubious means. The speakers are either parental figures, or "the sage," that is, the wisdom teacher who is addressing the audience, as at the beginning of chapter 5:

> *My child, to my wisdom pay attention,*
> *to my understanding incline your ear,*
> *so that you can maintain discretion,*
> *and so that your lips can guard knowledge.* (Proverbs 5:1–2)

Other topics in the first nine chapters include trusting God, staying on the optimal pathway, avoiding promiscuity, guarding the heart, and laziness, along with various binaries (e.g., light/dark, good/evil, life/death) and a chorus of voices that can lure one from the path of wisdom. Two major characters are Lady Wisdom and Lady Folly, and these characters represent the way of wisdom and paths of folly. When the reader arrives at chapter 9, there is a recognition that wisdom is accessible and desirable, and there is an invitation to a banquet in *her house of seven pillars*, suggesting there is ample room for everyone in this palatial temple:

> *She has sent out her maidens, she calls out from the tops of the city heights:*
> *"Whoever is simple, turn over here!" To anyone lacking in heart, she says:*
> *"Come, eat of my food and drink the wine I have mixed.*
> *Forsake your foolish ways and live,*
> *and go straight in the way of understanding."* (Proverbs 9:3–6)

The longest section of Proverbs, chapters 10–22, is a sprawling catalogue of brief poetic statements on an array of subjects. Examples include care for the poor, stewardship of creation and animals, gossip, friendship, and faithfulness. Sometimes these are stand-alone proverbs, but on other occasions there is the repetition of a keyword or idea with a neighboring proverb in order to create a more complex thought. Other subjects are money (pointing the reader toward an appreciation of what is truly valuable in life) and worry (illustrating the potential healing power of the spoken word), as in the following quotations:

> *Wealth has no profit in the day of wrath,*
> *But righteousness delivers from death.* (Proverbs 11:4)

> *Anxiety in someone's heart weighs it down,*
> *But a good word brings it joy.* (Proverbs 12:25)

Rather than absolute pronouncements, proverbs are better thought of as hard-earned poetic observations about how life works on the ground, and how to live with creativity and righteousness amidst lots of temptations. Diligence is commended (e.g., *those who work their land will have bread, but those who chase fantasies and empty schemes lack sense,* 12:11), avoiding folly is advised (e.g., *the simple inherit folly, but the prudent are crowned with knowledge,* 14:18), and self-control with one's speech and other actions should be a priority (e.g., *those who guard their mouth protect their lives, but those who open wide their lips come to ruin,* 13:3). The poetic technique found here is referred to as contrastive or antithetical parallelism, as two quite different outcomes are compared. Perhaps this explains why *the fear of the Lord* is mentioned so often (e.g., 8:13; 10:27; 14:26), emphasizing that every decision ought to be based on an awareness of God's character as the reader stands at a junction of the road, even in the midst of doubt or sorrow.

When reading wisdom texts after the Law and the Prophets, we notice that there is often a willingness to venture into some of the more troublesome and controversial areas of life, and there is a boldness to pose difficult questions about life's mysteries and frequent storms. Perhaps a portion of the wisdom literature emerged as a response to various crises in Israel's history—such as the exile—and helps the reader make sense of suffering while not abandoning the faith. There are occasions in the book of Proverbs when it feels like the setting in the garden of Eden is being revisited, where the choices between two trees (*the tree of the knowledge of good and evil* and *the tree of life*) that represent two different pathways in life are being placed before the reader. Indeed, wisdom is compared to a tree of life early in the book (3:18), and the idea of two ways is prominent throughout Proverbs (e.g., 14:12; 15:19). Near the center of the book there is a striking congruence of wisdom and the unique theology of Israel:

> *Through faithful love and truth, iniquity is atoned for,*
> *and by the fear of the Lord one turns aside from evil.* (Proverbs 16:6)

The rest of Proverbs consists of smaller collections, such as "the thirty sayings of the wise" (22:17 and following) or those copied by the court of Hezekiah (25:1). Again, the majority of these are short proverbs on topics seen elsewhere in the book, recognizing the need for discernment or learning from our mistakes. We know from other biblical texts that life may not always work out, and the poet of Psalm 73 complained that the wicked prosper while the righteous languish (cf. Jeremiah 12). But in general, the ancient sages would affirm that hard work will bring more benefits than laziness, and that cluelessness is not the best option for navigating life in a complex world. Numerous characters make an appearance in Proverbs to illustrate a certain point, and the *simple* are a case in point. Nowadays we might suggest that the simple (or naïve) are those who believe it when they are told: If you say "ice cream" really slow it sounds like "gullible." Proverbs 22:3 articulates a similar thought: *The shrewd see evil and hide themselves, but the simple walk right into it and get punished.*

Proverbs concludes with two collections from other sources. Agur speaks in chapter 30, while the otherwise unknown King Lemuel reflects on words that his mother taught him. In fact, the mother is given the final words in the book as she advises her son about the qualities of a noble wife: beauty is fleeting and charm is deceptive, but a woman who fears the Lord is highly praised (31:30). The entire book commences and climaxes with an invitation to fear God, which is the starting point and the endgame of the journey of wisdom.

Hour 38: Job 1–20

A POETIC DRAMA WITH suffering at its very heart, the book of Job has attracted a wide readership and much commentary over its long history. The story begins far away in the east, in the land of Uz: we are not exactly sure of Uz's location, other than it is not in Israel. Job, the main character, has been mentioned briefly by the prophet Ezekiel (14:14, 20). Various suggestions have been proposed for the meaning of Job's name—including *where is the father?* or *the enemy*—but these suggestions initially seem at odds with the immense wealth and ideal family that he enjoys in the opening sentences of the book. Notably, Job is characterized as a paragon of wisdom, one who fears God and turns aside from evil, even offering sacrifices on behalf of his children (who apparently enjoy feasting). It is hard to avoid the impression that Job's piety has paved the way for his great prosperity, but any notion of "faith equals blessings" is soon put to an eviscerating test.

Such testing starts abruptly, with a shift in setting and characters in 1:6 as the story moves from Job's idyllic life to the heavenly divine council. There are other occasions in the Bible where the reader briefly glimpses the throne room of God where the universe is governed (e.g., Isaiah 6; 1 Kings 22; Psalm 82), and here in Job 1 it appears to be a regularly scheduled meeting. Included among the powerful beings in this council chamber is *the Satan*, who seems to be roaming around in an adversarial role but is obligated to answer any question posed by God. One of those questions pertains to Job and his impressive piety, which elicits a story-changing response:

> *Then the Satan answered the Lord and said: "Does Job fear God sincerely? Haven't you built a fence around him and his house and everything he owns on every side? The work of his hands you've blessed, and the land is bursting with his possessions! But if you stretch out your hand and strike all that he owns, he will surely curse you to your face."* (Job 1:9–11)

The Satan's first question could also be translated: does Job fear God *for nothing* (that is, *for no gain*)? Job's motivation is the main point here, for it is insinuated that of course Job loves God because of all the bountiful things that have come his way! But take these things away, says the adversary, and Job will utter blasphemies in God's very presence. Whether the reader realizes it or not, this is a major theological moment—raised, of all figures, by the Satan—because by extension every believer is asked the same question: does your love for God come from who God is (that is, the divine majesty and character) or because of all the things God has given you?

For whatever reason, God grants permission (*Behold, all that he has is in your hand, but do not stretch out your hand against him*), as though agreeing to a wager. In casino terms, God goes "all in" on Job. A series of awful calamities are soon unleashed on the unsuspecting Job, destroying his oxen, sheep, camels, household staff, and even his children (1:13–19). At the end of this most tragic day, however, Job does not curse God, as the Satan said he would, despite all that has happened. There is also no hint that Job is aware of the divine council scene and God's conversation about him.

It is hard to fathom, but life gets even more unbearable for Job in chapter 2, which starts with another meeting of the divine council. The Satan makes another appearance, and God makes it clear that Job has maintained his integrity, counter to what the Satan insisted. But this adversary is relentless, and practically says "double or nothing" on the previous wager, and asserts that Job will curse God if his physical body is struck. Having been granted permission, Satan departs from the divine council *and he struck Job with evil boils from the soles of his feet to the crown of his head* (2:7). In Deuteronomy 28 the same term for "boils" is used in the context of a divine punishment for covenant unfaithfulness. Here in chapter 2 Job has now lost his wealth and his health. In fact, he's lost everything, except his wife, who (having also lost her children and possessions) tells him to curse God and die. Three of Job's friends arrive from distant places having heard the report, and burst into tears (2:12). For seven days they sit in silence, but as we will hear, they soon begin to speak.

So far in the book of Job we have been dealing with narrative prose, but chapter 3 and following are composed in poetry. There are hundreds of questions in the book of Job, each with varying degrees of difficulty, and perhaps poetry is the only medium for raising such painful inquiries about divine fairness and the problem of evil. Job is the first character to begin the long sequence of poetic dialogues, and in chapter 3 he unfurls a sevenfold curse *not* against God, but against the night of his conception and the day of his birth. At the very least, this poetry provides a different window on Job himself. The first two chapters are externally narrated, and the reader watches Job suffer. In the poetry, the perspective is now agonizingly internal, and we hear directly from his heart of sorrow: *for groaning arrives as my daily bread, my roaring pours out like water* (3:24).

Whether or not Job was intending to start an argument with his poetry in chapter 3, that is soon what happens, as the three friends abandon their posture of silence and unfurl long and virtually unfiltered responses to their miserable companion. In general, their poetic form can hardly be faulted, but their bedside manner is atrocious (to put it mildly). First up is Eliphaz in chapters 4–5, and perhaps he is the oldest, or has known Job the longest, but there is no indication as to why he opens the dialogue. But after seven days of silence Eliphaz seems in no mood to console: he is persuaded that *those who sow trouble reap the same* (4:8), and Job has been wounded as a kind of divine discipline. Job vigorously responds in chapters 6–7 by stating that the afflicted person should be able to count on the faithfulness of his friend (6:14), and that instead of keeping silent he will *complain in the bitterness of my soul* (7:11). When Bildad speaks up in chapter 8 with a cutting assertion about divine justice (*If your children sinned against him, then he gave them over into the hand of their transgression*, 8:4), Job responds in chapters 9–10 by saying that the innocent and the blameless are often treated poorly by God, who even smiles at the schemes of the wicked (10:3) despite having hand-crafted humanity in the divine image:

> *Your very hands fashioned me, and altogether made me,*
> *yet now you completely destroy me.*
> *Remember that you formed me as with clay,*
> *so now to the dust do you make me return?* (Job 10:8–9)

Of the three friends, Zophar uses slightly fewer words, but is equally convinced that somehow Job's sin lies at the root of his calamity, and this is probably why he says: *if iniquity is in your hand put it far away, and do not let unrighteousness live among your tents* (11:14). In a long response in chapters 12–14, Job continues to address God (*How many iniquities and sins do I have, let me know about my rebellion and my sin*, 13:23), igniting a second round of debate. With some variations, each of the friends maintains that Job's problems are connected to his actions, and even as they hold out hope for repentance and restoration, at some point Job will need to acknowledge his transgressions. For his part, Job declares his innocence even as he both calls to God and expresses his sorrow with passion and poignancy:

> *I was at peace but he shattered me, seized me by the neck,*
> *smashing me to pieces, setting me up as his target.*
> *His archers surround me, piercing my kidneys without mercy,*
> *my gall he pours out on the ground.*
> *Relentlessly he bursts forth against me,*
> *he rushes at me like a warrior.* (Job 16:12–14)

Hour 39: Job 21–42

There are lots of possible ideas about *when* the book of Job may have been written. It is set in a distant time and place—almost like the days of Abraham—but the language has affinities with later books of the Bible such as Lamentations. Perhaps the time of composition is during the exile when probing questions of suffering and divine justice reached a critical point. As we have seen so far, a central issue is the relationship between virtue and disastrous events. Eliphaz, Bildad, and Zophar are confident that there is a direct correlation between prosperity and piety, whereas Job—drawing on his own bitter experience—is questioning that certainty. Of course, if the friends are correct, then the wicked have to be miserable, which is why Zophar is persuaded that *the triumphant shout of the wicked is brief, and the joy of the profane lasts only a moment* (20:5). But in chapter 21 Job counters that the wicked often have a carefree life, and the calamities they deserve do not always befall them (21:17).

The final round of debate seems to be moving toward an impasse. Eliphaz sounds quite repetitive in chapter 22, although he does seem to compile an inventory of Job's sins: *Is not your evil vast, with no end to your iniquities?* (v. 5). Bildad is very brief but really angry in his last speech, and Zophar does not say anything at all. Job's concluding address to his friends includes the centerpiece of chapter 28, a hymn about wisdom that he might well be recalling as ancient tradition. Unlike gold and the finest of gems, wisdom cannot be extracted from the deepest recesses of the earth, nor can it be purchased with the most valuable of treasures. Rather, wisdom comes from God, and echoing the book of Proverbs, *the fear of the Lord is wisdom, and to turn aside from evil is understanding* (28:28). When Job's words resume in chapters 29–31, he unfolds a summary argument directed at the friends maintaining his own perception of innocence and calling for a divine audience:

Like Adam have I covered my transgressions,
hiding my iniquity within in my chest? ...

Oh, I wish there was someone to hear me!
Look at my signature, let the Almighty respond to me!
Oh, that I had the document written by my antagonist! (Job 31:33, 35)

With the long dialogue between Job and the three friends collapsing into an impasse, a previously unknown speaker suddenly emerges. Elihu has a recognizably Israelite name ("He is my God"), and straightaway we learn that he is younger, evidently listening the whole time and waiting for an opportunity to speak. Background details are not given, but clearly Elihu is hot with anger after hearing the various speeches. However, his own contribution begins with the admission—perhaps not the smartest move—that he is full of wind: *For I am full of words, the breath of my belly pushes on me. Behold, my belly is like unopened wine, like new wineskins about to burst out* (32:18–19). After hearing the core of his argument in chapters 33–36 the reader has to decide whether he is a wise voice from the periphery or a youthful bigmouth. Elihu finishes his speech in chapter 37 with images of divine majesty in the thunderclouds, and the voice of God that causes storm winds to depart.

Such references to clouds and lightning might signal that a storm has been brewing over the last few chapters. The particular term at the beginning of chapter 38 is used earlier, with just a very slight variation in spelling, by Job himself to describe his situation: *with a tempest he crushes me, and multiplies my wounds for no reason* (9:17). It also occurs in 2 Kings 2 when Elijah is swept up to heaven in a whirlwind replete with horses and a chariot of fire. Out of this tempest God's voice is now heard for the first time since the dialogue with the Satan at the beginning of this book. The reader might expect that God will start by explaining to Job about the wager at the outset and then respond to Job's myriad questions about suffering, the tragic fates of the innocent, and the fraught relationship between prosperity and piety. Any such answers, however, quickly take a backseat to God's opening words to Job in chapters 38–39. God asks him where he was when God laid the foundations of the earth (38:4), or if he has walked in the recesses of the deep (38:16), or contributed to the rich biodiversity of creation:

Is it through your understanding that the hawk soars,
spreading his wings toward the south?

At your command does the eagle mount up,
building his nest on high? (Job 39:26–27)

Near the beginning of chapter 40 Job speaks briefly, conceding that he can hardly answer because of his insignificance. But God continues and focuses attention on two particular creatures, *Behemoth* and *Leviathan*. On the one hand, some scholars interpret them as the hippopotamus and the crocodile, representing impressive animals from land and water. On the other hand, another option is to understand Behemoth and Leviathan as much more fearsome monsters. Equating Behemoth with the hippo is certainly a rational move, but perhaps at odds with description of 40:19 (*He was first in the ways of God, his maker can approach him with his sword*), implying the kind of power that only God can subdue. Leviathan appears earlier in 3:8 as an agent of chaotic destruction (cf. Isaiah 27:1), and descriptions such as 41:19 (*From his mouth come flaming torches, sparks of fire shooting forth*) and 41:23 (*he makes the deep boil like a cauldron*) indicate uncommon fierceness. Such descriptions from the divine voice elicit a final word from Job in 42:2–6 as he confesses that he spoke about things *too wonderful* and beyond his understanding.

After Job's final response to God, the poetry ends and there is a return narrative prose in the remainder of chapter 42 where Job is startlingly restored. As for Eliphaz and the two other friends who were convinced that Job was responsible for his own calamity, God's wrath is kindled and Job has to pray for them (young Elihu is not mentioned, for whatever reason). Job is given double his previous possessions and has ten new children, although we are not sure if his same wife is involved, and we are not told if Job rises early to present burnt offerings for these children just in case they have sinned and cursed God in their hearts (cf. 1:5). There is no indication that the Satan is anywhere present, nor is it clear if Job ever finds out what happened in the divine council behind the scenes with God's unshakable belief in Job. The book ends with the main character "old and full of years," but readers will spend the rest of their lives wrestling with these mysteries and trying to figure out how to serve God amidst the trials and vicissitudes of their remaining days, pondering the initial question about whether someone can love God *for who God is*, rather than because of various blessings that God has given (or things they hope God will give them).

Hour 40: Song of Songs

In many printed editions of the Hebrew Bible, the long story of Job is followed by a collection of five shorter books. Often called the "Five Festival Scrolls," in Jewish tradition each of these books is read during a particular occasion on the calendar: the *Song of Songs* is associated with Passover, *Ruth* with the feast of weeks or Pentecost, *Lamentations* on the ninth of Av commemorating the destruction of the Jerusalem temple, *Ecclesiastes* during the feast of Booths, and *Esther* with Purim (and the origins of this festival is the subject of the book itself). Perhaps bundling these five books together is a nod to the five books of the Torah or the Psalms. Regardless, each of these books has a distinct contribution to the overarching message of the Bible.

The first of the five scrolls to consider is the Song of Songs, which has the unique feature of being composed entirely of poetic speech. Also unusual is the absence of the divine name, although it is possible that 8:6 contains the short form of Yahweh (as in hallelu-*jah*): the NRSV translates 8:6 *raging flame*, but the ESV renders *as the very flame of the Lord*. Prominent throughout is a remarkable female voice, describing everything from her beloved to the landscape in lush and luxurious terms. Such a perspective has led some to conclude that the author is a woman, while others maintain Solomonic authorship in the same tradition as Proverbs and Ecclesiastes. The title "Song of Songs" is a superlative expression that implies "the ultimate song," much like "king of kings" implies the ultimate king or "holy of holies" the most sacred place. So, we could think of the title as *the best of songs about Solomon*, and one of the many puzzles is figuring out the role of Israel's notorious king in this book. Straightaway, the opening lines plunge the reader into the sensuous world of this lyric poetry:

Let him kiss me with the kisses of his mouth,

for your love is better than wine.
The scent of your oils is most pleasing,
your name is like oil poured out,
this is why all the maidens love you! (Song of Songs 1:2–3)

There is no proper name ascribed to the woman in the Song of Songs, but in 6:13 she is referred as the *Shulammite*; maybe this is a village, but more likely it is the feminine form of Solomon's name. As we recall from 1 Kings 11, Solomon infamously had 1,000 wives (note the allusion in 8:12–13), so perhaps the reader is invited to imagine the woman as a faithful foil to royal harem (e.g., 6:8–10). Indeed, it sounds like she is pledged to the male character in the song, and hence the alternating voices that can be heard throughout. Just as the woman elaborately compares her lover to towering cedar trees and marble columns, so the male declares that the hair of his beloved is like a flock of goats descending from Mount Gilead and that her lips drip with sweetness like the honeycomb. We can hear both voices going back and forth at the beginning of chapter 2:

I am a rose of Sharon, a lily of the valleys.

As a lily among brambles,
so is my girlfriend among the young women.

Like an apple tree among the trees of the forest,
so is my beloved among the boys,
In his shade I take great delight,
and his fruit is sweet to my taste. (Song of Songs 2:1–3)

One of the perennial questions about this book is whether it has the semblance of a plot, or whether it is an assortment of love lyrics compiled over a period of time. Furthermore, the history of interpretation is not without controversy. By far the most common approach, interestingly enough, is the allegorical approach: that is, viewing thesong as ultimately a celebration of God's love for Israel (and by extension, Christ's love for the church). On the one hand, there is ample marriage imagery in prophetic material that illustrate God's love and commitment, as opposed to the covenant unfaithfulness of the people. Examples include Isaiah 62:5 (*As a son-in-law rejoices over the bride, your God will rejoice over you*) and Hosea 2:14 (*I will allure her and lead her into the wilderness*). Moreover, the New Testament includes such images, as in 2 Corinthians 11:2, Ephesians 5:22–32, and assorted references in Revelation 18–22. On the other hand, the passages just cited always make the connection between God and humanity explicit, whereas there is no such indication in the song.

Also, in order to work allegorically, some passages would also need a quite fanciful interpretation. When considering the vivid description of Solomon's retinue, it might pose a challenge to discern a transcendent spiritual sense:

What is this coming up from the wilderness like columns of smoke?
. . .
Behold, it is the roving couch of Solomon,
with sixty men around it, from the warriors of Israel.
All of them skilled with the sword, experienced in warfare,
each has a sword at his side, because of the terrors of night. (Song of Songs 3:6–8)

More popular in recent years is the romantic interpretation. The plethora of intimate details enhanced by an array of images from the natural landscape along with items of clothing and jewelry combine to form a rich celebration of human love. To what extent the various scenes might represent dreams or imaginative longings continue to be debated among scholars. There are other views of the song that understand it as a kind of drama of faithfulness: the maiden is tempted to consider the court of Solomon with all of its opulence, but in the end chooses to honor her fiancé. Some commentators suggest the song—in whole or in parts—would have been recited or performed at weddings (compare Psalm 45), which makes sense of the chorus that appears several times in the book. Still others maintain that the song was included in the canon of Scripture because it underscores delight in God's creation of human intimacy, with wise advice about various dangers, boundaries, and the surpassing value of love:

O daughters of Jerusalem, I want you to swear an oath,
by the gazelles or the does of the field,
Do not stir up or awaken love until it is pleased. (Song of Songs 2:7)

Many waters are not able to extinguish love,
rivers cannot float it away.
If someone offered all the riches of his house for love,
it would be utterly scorned. (Song of Songs 8:7)

Hour 41: Ruth

In the Christian Bible the book of Ruth is placed between Judges and 1 Samuel, providing another angle on the narrative as the nation moves toward the monarchy. But in Hebrew tradition, as mentioned, Ruth is located in the Writings, and read aloud during the Feast of Weeks fifty days after Passover. The opening sentence, *In the days when the judges were judging*, situates the story during the often chaotic period when there was no king in Israel, and *everyone did what was upright in their own eyes* (Judges 21:25). Geographically, the book begins in Bethlehem of Judah—the hometown of David according to 1 Samuel 16—and focuses on the family of Elimelech ("my God is king"), his wife Naomi ("pleasant"), and their sons Mahlon ("sick") and Chilion ("destruction"). A famine prompts this family to relocate to Moab, an abrasive neighboring country, and with echoes of Abraham they depart from the land because of an emergency.

It is unclear how long this family was planning to stay, although the marriages of the two sons imply a longer sojourn. But Elimelech dies, as do Mahlon and Chilion, perhaps not surprising given the meaning of their names. Bereft in a foreign land, Naomi hears that God has provided food for his people (1:6) and she begins her homeward journey. In the longest scene of the chapter, Orpah (gazelle) and Ruth (friendship) declare that they will accompany her, but Naomi directs them to remain within their own land. Orpah chooses to stay, but Ruth clings to her mother-in-law: *where you go, I will go . . . your people will be my people, and your God, my God* (1:16). Upon their arriving in Bethlehem, the town is abuzz, but Naomi insists that her name is now *Marah* ("bitter") as she unleashes a torrent of Job-like inner emotion about her fate to the local women:

> *Don't call me Naomi anymore, call me Marah, because the Almighty has dealt bitterly with me. I was full when I went away, but the Lord*

> *has brought me back empty. Why would you call me "Naomi," for the Lord has testified against me, and the Almighty has brought evil upon me?* (Ruth 1:21)

At the end of chapter 1 the barley harvest is just beginning, enabling Ruth to scour the fields and find enough food for her and Naomi to survive at the start of chapter 2. Leviticus 19:9–10 teaches that Israelite landowners should leave behind the fallen grapes of the vineyard so they can be picked up by the poor and the foreign refugees. This teaching hovers in the background here, but it also underscores the dismal situation of Naomi and Ruth. It also illustrates Ruth's commitment to her mother-in-law as she scavenges in this field. However, *by chance* (the Hebrew expresses a lucky surprise) it just happens to be a field that belongs to a relative of Elimelech's named Boaz ("strength"). Boaz is introduced as a *man of valor*, and after noticing Ruth in his field, clearly does some investigating and soon speaks words of affirmation to her:

> *Everything that you've done for your mother-in-law since the death of your husband has been told to me, and how you left your father, mother and the land of your birth, and came to a people that you did not know beforehand. May the Lord reward you for your efforts, and may your wages be complete from the Lord God of Israel, who you have come to take refuge beneath his wings!* (Ruth 2:11–12)

In the aftermath of the Song of Songs, any flirtatious dynamic here in chapter 2 seems quite mild. But Boaz is aware of her Moabite status and her widowhood, even as his spiritual language is very inclusive toward this outsider. When Ruth returns to her mother-in-law with a considerable amount of grain—much more than could be expected from merely gleaning for leftovers in the field—Naomi senses that *someone* has taken notice of Ruth. Upon learning that Boaz has dispensed the grain to Ruth, her tone is a joyful contrast with her earlier lament about the bitterness of God's treatment: *May he be blessed by the Lord, who has not abandoned his covenant faithfulness to the living or the dead!* (2:20). Sounding a lot less like Job, Naomi reveals that Boaz is a relative, and also brings up the idea of the "kinsman redeemer" (*go'el*). In the case of a premature death, Deuteronomy 25:5–10 states that a close relative of the deceased should act to preserve the family's name and property through marriage and/or money. Naomi appears to be assuming the principle of the kinsman redeemer, and this fuels the next installment of the story.

Once the harvest is over—and perhaps Naomi's situation is even more precarious—she slyly suggests that Ruth needs to seek out a better situation at the outset of chapter 3. Does she now believe that an unseen divine hand is at work behind the chance meeting in the field of Boaz? Regardless, she knows exactly what Boaz is doing that evening (3:2–4), and in what looks like an elaborate ancient Near Eastern dating ritual, instructs Ruth to *uncover his feet* when he is sleeping on the grain pile. Awakening with a start, Boaz figures things out, but explains that there is a relative closer than him who has the first obligation to Naomi's family (3:12). But he also pledges to resolve the matter straightaway, and as Ruth returns to her mother-in-law with a load of barley, Boaz heads to the city gate where legal business is conducted (Deuteronomy 22:15).

With a sense of urgency, chapter 4 begins with Boaz at the gate and the almost simultaneous entrance of the relative who is closer in line to Elimelech. This relative is labeled as "Mr. So & So." Since it feels like the Bible has about one million proper names, the absence of a name here suggest that this figure is negatively characterized. Indeed, when Boaz presents the situation, he immediately agrees, but when he finds out that he won't personally profit from this transaction (since he has to marry Ruth; is he anti-Moabite?). Mr. So & So declines his responsibility: we never learn his name because his chance for biblical fame has been erased due to his own self-centered actions (4:6). Meanwhile, Boaz confirms the transaction by removing his sandal (see Deuteronomy 25:9–10 for a more shocking example), marrying Ruth and thus reviving the line of Elimelech, because in due course she gives birth to a son. The women of the town speak once more, and like a chorus they express the joy of Naomi:

> *"Blessed be the Lord, who has not left you this day without next-of-kin; and may his name be renowned in Israel! He shall be to you a restorer of life and a nourisher of your old age; for your daughter-in-law who loves you, who is more to you than seven sons, has borne him."* (Ruth 4:14–15, NRSV)

The book ends with a genealogy in 4:18–22, and it is a vital one as the climactic name at the end is *David*. It turns out, therefore, that Ruth is the great-grandmother of none other than Israel's most celebrated king. Despite her status as a Moabite outsider, she is engrafted into the royal line of Israel, and perhaps this is why the book is read in Jewish tradition during the Feast of Ingathering (see Acts 2 for a New Testament celebration of that harvest festival). Speaking of the New Testament, Ruth's name is found on the opening page of Matthew's Gospel, and becomes a remarkable foreshadowing of discipleship, covenant commitment, and the integration of the marginalized into the vast family of God's people.

Hour 42: Lamentations

It would be difficult to overstate the effect of the temple's destruction and the demise of Jerusalem on the people of God, and its implications can be perceived in a considerable percentage of biblical material. Narrated in 2 Kings 25 and reiterated in Jeremiah 52, the invasion at the hands of the Babylonian army is tersely recorded. But other poetic and prophetic texts are not so reserved: Isaiah 24:13 pictures a beaten and bare olive tree, Ezekiel 5 graphically includes a shaved head and a sword when describing the siege and capture of Jerusalem, and Psalm 74:7–8 painfully outlines the burning of the divine dwelling place. In the aftermath of this assault, another response to the traumatic event is Lamentations. As is evident from the opening lines, there is empty desolation as the poet surveys a ruined world:

How lonely sits the city
that once was full of people!
How like a widow she has become,
she that was great among the nations!
She that was a princess among the provinces
has become a vassal.
She weeps bitterly in the night,
with tears on her cheeks;
among all her lovers
she has no one to comfort her;
all her friends have dealt treacherously with her,
they have become her enemies. (Lamentations 1:1–2 NRSV)

Lamentations has different locations in Scripture: in Christian tradition, following the Greek Septuagint, it is placed after Jeremiah, whereas it is part of the Writings and the fourth of the Five Festival Scrolls in the Hebrew Bible. While the authorship is anonymous, it has long been maintained that Jeremiah is the author because of his reputation as the "weeping prophet" and the seemingly eyewitness testimony of the book. On the other hand, much of the poetry is a different style than Jeremiah's, and the immersive feel does not necessarily demand someone in close proximity. But it certainly is a poet like Jeremiah, who emotively identifies with the onslaught and devastation of Jerusalem.

> *Is it nothing to you, all you who pass by?*
> *Look and see if there is any sorrow like my sorrow,*
> *which was brought upon me, which the Lord inflicted*
> *on the day of his fierce anger.*
> *From on high he sent fire; it went deep into my bones;*
> *he spread a net for my feet; he turned me back;*
> *he has left me stunned, faint all day long.* (Lamentations 1:12–13 NRSV)

The book is structured as a sequence of five chapters, with each chapter being an individual poem. An acrostic style is used in the first four poems, with the twenty-two letters of the Hebrew alphabet successively appearing in the stanzas of each poem. We have noticed the acrostic form previously in Psalm 119 and Proverbs 31:10–21. Here, most scholars suggest that the acrostic style is used to emphasize the completeness of the catastrophe, that is, an A-to-Z inventory of mourning and woe in light of this misery. Various kinds of voices can be heard, and there are shifts in perspective at numerous points throughout the poems. The genre of lament is seen frequently in the Psalms, and it might be worth comparing David's eulogy for Saul and Jonathan as a similar genre that expresses individual and corporate suffering because of war:

> *O hills of Gilboa, may you not have dew,*
> *May rain not fall on you, O fields of sacrifice.*
> *For there the shield of heroes was defiled,*
> *The shield of Saul not anointed with oil.*
> *From the blood of the slain,*
> *From the flesh of the warriors,*
> *The bow of Jonathan did not retreat,*
> *The sword of Saul did not return empty.* (2 Samuel 2:21–22)

There is an acknowledgment of guilt in chapter 1, and the poet confesses to a churning stomach because of rebellion and admits that these disasters have arrived because of manifest transgressions. But in chapter 2 there is an aggressive expression of anger, as God becomes the subject of numerous verbs of destruction. Divine actions include laying waste the strongholds of Judah and bending his bow like an enemy, as wrath is poured out like fire and the walls of Zion are razed to the ground. Chapter 3 is the most visually complex of the five poems, and at times has a stream-of-consciousness style that immerses the reader in the dark and lonely journey into exile. However, the most famous verses occur in the center of chapter 3, which is also the center of the entire book, a bold declaration of comfort in the midst of the greatest sorrow:

> *The thought of my affliction and my homelessness*
> *is wormwood and gall!*
> *My soul continually thinks of it*
> *and is bowed down within me.*
> *But this I call to mind,*
> *and therefore I have hope:*
> *The steadfast love of the Lord never ceases,*
> *his mercies never come to an end;*
> *they are new every morning;*
> *great is your faithfulness.* (Lamentations 3:19–23, NRSV)

Alongside the central affirmation of God's covenant fidelity (*hesed*) at the midpoint of the book, chapters 4–5 nonetheless continue the earlier themes, including a grim comparison to the overthrow of Sodom (4:6) and a haunting description of wandering the empty streets covered only in blood-stained garments (4:14), along with calls for accountability of the perpetrators (5:1) and desperate privations in the ruined land (5:8–16). Notably, the book ends with an open-ended statement of grief. On the one hand, the final lines take responsibility for a litany of covenant failures on the part of God's people, but on the other hand, they express a willingness to call out for divine mercy and express hopes for restoration that utterly depend on an initiative of grace:

> *But you, O Lord, reign forever;*
> *your throne endures to all generations.*
> *Why have you forgotten us completely?*
> *Why have you forsaken us these many days?*
> *Restore us to yourself, O Lord,*
> *that we may be restored;*
> *renew our days as of old—*
> *unless you have utterly rejected us,*
> *and are angry with us beyond measure.* (Lamentations 5:19–22, NRSV)

Hour 43: Ecclesiastes

If the Bible has a midlife crisis, then Ecclesiastes might be a prime candidate. From the opening speech and onwards, there is a relentless reflection on the meaning of life in a world of frustrating schemes and futile ventures. Regardless of how the first key line is translated (*Vanity of vanities, saith the Preacher* in the old KJV, or *"Meaningless! Meaningless!" says the Teacher* in the NRSV), the reader immediately gets the impression that this book will not be filled with cliché. The Hebrew term translated as vanity or meaningless is *hebel*, and it is first seen in Genesis 4 as the name of Cain's brother "Abel." As we recall, in that story Abel's life is cut short after a senseless act of brutality. While the term is difficult to pin down, in Isaiah 57:13 it refers to a fleeting vapor, and in 2 Kings 17:15 *vanity* is used to describe useless idols as a cause of the nation's downfall. Overall, this same word for vanity in Ecclesiastes speaks to the ultimate futility of human life and labor without any stable foundation.

Hebrew tradition refers to this book as *Qoheleth*, based on the main speaking character that is rendered by some standard English translations as "the Preacher." This figure is often thought to be Solomon on the basis of the opulent landscapes in the first two chapters. However, the first sentence of the book identifies the speaker as *a descendant of David* who ruled in Jerusalem, and so perhaps Qoheleth is a representative character who reflects on the collapse of kingship and related endeavors in light of the exile. Other translations such as the NIV and NRSV opt for "the Teacher," probably on the basis of the closing epilogue in chapter 12 that mentions teaching knowledge to the community, and studying many proverbs (12:9). Linguistic analysis suggests that certain words such as "parks" in 2:5 are of Persian origin, and perhaps hint at a date of composition after the exile. Regardless, the reader is immediately invited to consider a programmatic question that casts its shadow over the entire book: "*What is the profit for someone from all the toil at which they toil under the sun?* (Ecclesiastes 1:3).

Echoes of life outside of Eden in the initial discourse about toil and profitless undertakings have a tone of frustration, and if the book is composed after the exile, that sense of frustration could be directed at that the monumental failure of the nation's kings. This could be why the opening chapters unfold a lengthy review of Israel's royal enterprise: "*I, the Preacher, have been king over Israel in Jerusalem, and I applied my mind to seek and to search out with wisdom concerning all that has been done under heaven*" (Ecclesiastes 1:12–13). A monarchic experiment of probing the grand projects of the past start with what certainly looks like the Solomonic kingdom with all of its extravagant indulgence:

> *I made great works; I built houses and planted vineyards for myself; I made myself gardens and parks, and planted in them all kinds of fruit trees. I made myself pools from which to water the forest of growing trees. I bought male and female slaves, and had slaves who were born in my house; I also had great possessions of herds and flocks, more than any who had been before me in Jerusalem. I also gathered for myself silver and gold and the treasure of kings and of the provinces; I got singers, both men and women, and delights of the flesh, and many concubines.* (Ecclesiastes 2:4–8 NRSV)

Allusion to Solomon is quite clear in this section, but the persona gradually fades and other memories come into view. Probably the most famous lines in the book are at the beginning of chapter 3, and they have even been memorialized in pop songs of the twentieth century: *There is a season for everything, and a time for all that is done under heaven* (Ecclesiastes 3:1). This poetic reflection about times and seasons might be referring to an inventory of typical life experience, or alternatively, might be a compact summary of the vicissitudes of Israel's royal history. Journalists frequently note that history may not repeat itself, but it certainly does rhyme. Along these lines is an anecdote about monarchic succession that underscores how easy it is to succumb to a reign of folly, and how quickly people forget the lessons of the past in pursuit of vanity:

> *Better is a poor but wise youth than an old but foolish king, who will no longer take advice. One can indeed come out of prison to reign, even though born poor in the kingdom. I saw all the living who, moving about under the sun, follow that youth who replaced the king; there was no end to all those people whom he led. Yet those*

> *who come later will not rejoice in him. Surely this also is vanity and a chasing after wind.* (Ecclesiastes 4:13–15 NRSV)

Interpreters over the centuries have lodged various complaints about what is perceived to be Qoheleth's pessimistic or skeptical stance. Along with some apparent contradictions, there is no shortage of challenges for the reader. Here is a typical example: *All the labor of humanity is for their mouth, and yet the appetite is never satisfied. For what is the advantage that the wise have compared to the fool? What do the poor know about the walk of life?* (Ecclesiastes 6:7–8). It could be argued that an intentional rhetorical strategy is at work, and perhaps Qoheleth is subjecting every aspect of Israelite tradition—wisdom included—to a stringent test in order to evaluate what is the best way to move forward in an uncertain world. It is worth pointing out that in Jewish tradition the book of Ecclesiastes is read during the Feast of Booths (Ex 23:16; Deut 16:13–15), perhaps as an acknowledgment of the "wilderness" aspect of human existence and gratitude for the harvest.

Another matter that is raised more than once is joy, and the admonition to take simple pleasure in the gifts of food and drink: "*You who are young, be happy while you are young, and let your heart give you joy in the days of your youth. Follow the ways of your heart and whatever your eyes see, but know that for all these things God will bring you into judgment. So then, banish anxiety from your heart and cast off the troubles of your body, for youth and vigor are meaningless*" (Ecclesiastes 11:9–10 NIV). Indeed, this directive to the next generation is part of the larger conclusion that speaks to a younger population. Included in the conclusion is a return to the editorial voice heard at the outset of the book, with an emphasis of a key themes in wisdom literature (*The end of the matter, after all has been heard: Fear God, and keep his commands, for this is the whole of humanity,* 12:13). Similarly, Qoheleth's closing words ought to be prioritized in the reader's mind:

> *Remember your creator in the days of your youth, before the days of trouble come, and the years draw near when you will say, "I have no pleasure in them"; before the sun and the light and the moon and the stars are darkened and the clouds return with the rain . . . and the dust returns to the earth as it was, and the breath returns to God who gave it. Vanity of vanities, says the Teacher; all is vanity.* (Ecclesiastes 12:1–2; 7–8, NRSV)

Hour 44: Esther

King Xerxes might be better known to a generation of moviegoers as the Persian king in the days of the movie *300*. But the book of Esther presents a rather different portrait of that monarch, also referred to as Ahasuerus (Ezra 4:6). This short story is set deep in the heart of the Persian Empire and its capital city of Susa, during the postexilic period in the mid-fifth century BCE. The first sentence of the narrative (*This is what occurred during the days of Xerxes, the Xerxes who reigned over 127 provinces stretching from India to Cush*) sets the stage for an outrageous 180-day banquet in the most lavish of spatial locations. It might be hard to believe that a problem could arise in this setting, but if the book includes a satirical feel, then Queen Vashti's refusal to come when summoned by the king (1:12) precipitates a crisis. After consulting with his lawyers, Xerxes deposes his queen, but upon (soberly) reflecting on his actions the next day, seems terrified to be single. An empire-wide search for a new queen is undertaken, and among the many candidates is the main character of this story:

> *Now there was in the citadel of Susa a Jew of the tribe of Benjamin, named Mordecai son of Jair, the son of Shimei, the son of Kish, who had been carried into exile from Jerusalem by Nebuchadnezzar king of Babylon, among those taken captive with Jehoiachin king of Judah. Mordecai had a cousin named Hadassah, whom he had brought up because she had neither father nor mother. This young woman, who was also known as Esther, had a lovely figure and was beautiful. Mordecai had taken her as his own daughter when her father and mother died.* (Esther 2:5–7 NIV)

From a wide pool of candidates, in due course Esther is chosen to be queen in place of Vashti. For some reason Mordecai instructs her to keep her Jewish identity a secret; incidentally, the name Esther sounds like the Hebrew word for "I have concealed." At the end of chapter 2 Mordecai somehow uncovers a conspiracy to assassinate the king, the perpetrators are hanged, and a record of this deed is noted in the royal archives.

Meanwhile, at the start of chapter 3 there is the introduction of a new character freshly promoted by the king: Haman the Agagite. In 1 Samuel 15 "Agag" is an Amalekite king, implying that Haman is a descendant of Israel's perennial foe. Ever since the unprovoked attack of the Amalekites in Exodus 17 there has been bitter animosity between these two groups, and now the ancient rivalry is revived on this Persian stage. Presumably this is why Mordecai refuses to bow before the promoted Haman, kindling the wrath of the wealthy Amalekite:

> *When Haman saw that Mordecai would not kneel down or pay him honor, he was enraged. Yet having learned who Mordecai's people were, he scorned the idea of killing only Mordecai. Instead Haman looked for a way to destroy all Mordecai's people, the Jews, throughout the whole kingdom of Xerxes. In the twelfth year of King Xerxes, in the first month, the month of Nisan, the* pur *(that is, the lot) was cast in the presence of Haman to select a day and month. And the lot fell on the twelfth month, the month of Adar.* (Esther 3:5–7 NIV)

With him confident in his scheme, the *pur* is cast before Haman prior to asking permission from the king. As it turns out, the dice is rolled during an auspicious time: the month of Nisan is traditionally the month of Passover, and so the casting of the *pur* coincides with the annual celebration of deliverance from genocide and Egyptian slavery. Perhaps knowing that the king does not like any kind of insubordination, Haman declares that a subversive people group needs to be eliminated, and coupled with the offer of a vast sum of money, an empire-wide edict of destruction is soon issued. Upon hearing the news, Mordecai is distraught, and after some dialogue with Esther, he presents her with a challenge:

> *When Esther's words were reported to Mordecai, he sent back this answer: "Do not think that because you are in the king's house you alone of all the Jews will escape. For if you remain silent at this time, relief and deliverance for the Jews will arise from another place, but you and your father's family will perish. And who knows but that you have come to your royal position for such a time as this?"* (Esther 4:12–14 NIV)

Taking a grave risk, Esther approaches the king without an appointment at the beginning of chapter 5, and unlike her predecessor Vashti, Esther's boldness is rewarded with the king's extended scepter. Esther invites the king—along with Haman—to a banquet she has prepared, although when the feasting king then asks about her request (5:6), she proceeds to invite them both again to *another* banquet on the following day when she will reveal her request. Haman is buoyed by these honors, but then glum when he sees an unbowed Mordecai at the city gate. His wife and friends suggest that Haman build a gallows seventy-five feet high to hang his enemy, and delighted with this idea, Haman orders that the gallows be erected and proceeds to ask for the king's permission to execute Mordecai.

However, Xerxes happens to be suffering from insomnia on that very night, and has the reports of the royal archive read aloud to him. In these reports he hears about the incident where Mordecai uncovered the assassination plot, and yet no reward was given. It turns out that Haman is lurking around, and when the king asks about a reward for *one whom the king delights to honor*, Haman naturally concludes that it is him, and quickly unfurls a lengthy list of accolades. By all means do all of this, the king orders, to Mordecai the Jew who sits at the king's gate. Haman has to comply, no doubt with gritted teeth and seething resentment, and there follows a curious and ominous scene:

> *Then Mordecai returned to the king's gate, but Haman hurried to his house, mourning and with his head covered. When Haman told his wife Zeresh and all his friends everything that had happened to him, his advisers and his wife Zeresh said to him, "If Mordecai, before whom your downfall has begun, is of the Jewish people, you will not prevail against him, but will surely fall before him." While they were still talking with him, the king's eunuchs arrived and hurried Haman off to the banquet that Esther had prepared.* (Esther 6:12–14 NRSV)

At the banquet of chapter 7 the story reaches its climax as Esther finally shares her petition with the king, and with a deft combination of flattery and passion, reveals that *her people* are the target of the edict of annihilation that Haman has orchestrated. Realizing his dire predicament, Haman is full of fear, although when the king departs to cool off in the garden, Haman has one last chance: begging for his life, Haman approaches the queen and throws himself down before her, in a parody of the scenes where Mordecai refuses to bow. But the timing could not be worse, as the still furious king reenters that room at that very moment:

> *When the king returned from the palace garden to the banquet hall, Haman had thrown himself on the couch where Esther was reclining;*

> *and the king said, "Will he even assault the queen in my presence, in my own house?" As the words left the mouth of the king, they covered Haman's face. Then Harbona, one of the eunuchs in attendance on the king, said, "Look, the very gallows that Haman has prepared for Mordecai, whose word saved the king, stands at Haman's house, fifty cubits high." And the king said, "Hang him on that." So they hanged Haman on the gallows that he had prepared for Mordecai. Then the anger of the king abated.* (Esther 7:8–10 NRSV)

When Haman is hanged on the very gallows that he built for Mordecai, there is an ironic reversal that carries echoes of Exodus. Indeed, just as Pharaoh and the Egyptians tried to drown the Israelites in Exodus 1, so a later king and the Egyptian army are drowned in the waters of the Red Sea in Exodus 14. As hinted earlier, there are a number of other allusions to the wider Exodus story: both Moses and Esther are adopted and have strategic names, the *pur* is cast in the same month as Passover, a new feast is inaugurated and named Purim, Haman's house is plundered much like the Egyptians were plundered, and the genocidal decree is nullified and sealed with a celebration. Other reversals are seen in chapters 8–10 with the promotion of Mordecai, but most readers will notice the absence of any divine name in the book. Perhaps God is active in the book of Esther, but behind the scenes, and the placement of Esther among the Writings of the Hebrew invite the community to use wisdom in order to discern God at work in the world.

Hour 45: Daniel

In most Christian Bibles the book of Daniel is located among the prophetic literature, right after Ezekiel and before the Minor Prophets. But in the Hebrew Bible the book is found after the Five Festival Scrolls and immediately before Ezra-Nehemiah. Notably, there are two languages used in Daniel, with chapters 1 and 8–12 written in classical Hebrew, while most of chapters 2–7 are written in Aramaic. There are different scholarly views on the date of composition, with some seeing an earlier date, while many others view the book as a second-century BCE document written as a response to the crises of that period. The main narrative begins with the first wave of exilic captives, prior to the invasion and destruction of Jerusalem. Overall, the story encourages wise living in uncertain times, along with faithfulness in times of trial. There are two main parts to the book: chapters 1–6 take place in the Babylonian court over a considerable period of time, while chapters 7–12 present a series of visions that Daniel experiences in a foreign land.

The book opens with a traumatic event: *In the third year of the reign of Jehoiakim king of Judah, Nebuchadnezzar king of Babylon came and besieged Jerusalem.* Along with the temple vessels, Daniel and his three friends are included in the group of deported captives (cf. 2 Kings 24:14), and enrolled in a training program where they are given new names that signal a desire for them to shift their loyalties to the empire. But the temptation to assimilate is resisted by these young men, who are given unique wisdom—an important theme in the book—and the final line of the chapter suggests that they outlast the very empire responsible for their exile (1:21). The king of Babylon is mentioned in the first verse of the book, and in chapter 2 he has a dream like Pharaoh in the days of Joseph in Genesis. But Nebuchadnezzar refuses to share the content of his dream with his court magicians, and demands that they tell him both the content and the meaning of the dream. Their inability contrasts with Daniel's prayer for divine insight, and God reveals both the royal dream and its implications: a tall statue representing the kingdoms of the earth actually has feet of clay, and is struck by a great rock:

> *And in the days of those kings the God of heaven will set up a kingdom that shall never be destroyed, nor shall this kingdom be left to another people. It shall crush all these kingdoms and bring them to an end, and it shall stand forever; just as you saw that a stone was cut from the mountain not by hands, and that it crushed the iron, the bronze, the clay, the silver, and the gold. The great God has informed the king what shall be hereafter. The dream is certain, and its interpretation trustworthy.* (Daniel 2:44–45 NRSV)

Nebuchadnezzar's response to Daniel's words at the end of chapter 2 is to acknowledge the superiority of this God, and further promote the young men from Judah. Daniel remains at the court, with the three friends appointed to administrative posts in the province of Babylon. Despite his dream of a powerful statue that ultimately is unstable, at the start of chapter 3 the king builds a ninety-foot gold statue. At the unveiling ceremony there is a stern order: whoever does not bow down in worship when the music plays will face the penalty of death by incineration. When the noncompliance of Shadrach, Meshach, and Abednego is reported, the king's wrath is kindled, and yet they are filled with composure: *O Nebuchadnezzar, we have no need to present a defense to you in this matter. If our God whom we serve is able to deliver us from the furnace of blazing fire and out of your hand, O king, let him deliver us. But if not, be it known to you, O king, that we will not serve your gods and we will not worship the golden statue that you have set up* (3:16–18, NRSV). Although the furnace is heated up seven times hotter when the lads are thrown in, the king leaps to feet when seeing them alive and accompanied by a fourth figure of dazzling appearance. Once more the king is prompted to declare the supremacy of God, and the chapter ends with the three youngsters, who emerge from this ordeal with their faith unscathed, again promoted in the royal regime.

Chapter 4 begins with a first-person reminiscence of Nebuchadnezzar as he recounts a dream, the failure of his court magicians to interpret it, and once more the successful intervention of Daniel: he explains that the dream of the tree is a picture of the king himself, who is warned about a dire humbling. The rest of the chapter details how the king does not take this warning seriously (*Is this not magnificent Babylon, which I have built as a royal capital by my mighty power and for my glorious majesty?*, 4:30, NRSV) and ends up eating grass with long fingernails. The king does eventually acknowledge the sovereignty of God, and his experience is not unlike the exiles of Judah: disobedience, followed by a chastisement, but then a restoration that comes with a fresh recognition that divine authority transcends that of any empire. But Nebuchadnezzar is soon out of the picture as Belshazzar takes center stage at the start of chapter 5, and he orders that the sacred vessels of the Jerusalem temple be brought forth so that he and his circle of friends might drink from them. As they are praising various gods, an uninvited guest shows up:

> *Immediately the fingers of a human hand appeared and began writing on the plaster of the wall of the royal palace, next to the lampstand. The king was watching the hand as it wrote. Then the king's face turned pale, and his thoughts terrified him. His limbs gave way* [lit. the knots of his loins were loosened], *and his knees knocked together.* (Daniel 5:5–6 NRSV)

As the bracketed translation above indicates, the Aramaic text reveals that the king's clothing was soiled as he lost control of his bowels because of fear of the disembodied hand that suddenly appears. No one can read the writing on the wall, until Daniel is called and interprets the meaning of the words: Belshazzar has been weighed and found wanting, and the kingdom will be divided. As it turns out, this is a dismal night for the Babylonian Empire: *That very night Belshazzar, the Chaldean king, was killed. And Darius the Mede received the kingdom, being about sixty-two years old* (5:30–31 NRSV).

With Belshazzar slain, chapter 6 begins with Darius and his effort to reorganize the administration. The promotion of Daniel, though, provokes jealousy among the other leaders, and Darius is soon swayed into signing a document making it illegal to pray to anyone except the king. Daniel continues his customary practice of prayer to God (6:10; cf. Psalm 55:17), and when charges are brought, the king has no choice but to order that Daniel be thrown into a den of lions. Anxiously, Darius fasts all night before hurrying to the den at daybreak and calling out, only to hear Daniel's response that he is alive and well, courtesy of a divine angel who prevented any harm. When the conspirators themselves are then thrown into the lion's den as punishment, there is sense of measure-for-measure retribution, and the chapter ends with another decree that all must tremble and fear before the God of Daniel.

The second part of the book, chapters 7–12, starts with a vision from the period of Belshazzar, and includes Daniel's personal recounting of a dream of four great beasts that came out of the sea. After descriptions of these four terrifying monsters, the scene shifts to the divine court (7:9–10) presided over by the ancient of days. Another key figure is *one like a son of man* who is given authority taken away from the beasts. If the four beasts represent a series of empires, then it is notable that the dominion of *the son of man* is everlasting, with a kingdom that will never be destroyed (7:13–14). Previously in the book, Daniel is the interpreter of royal dreams, but now he needs interpretation. When he asks a nearby attendant, it is confirmed that the beast represents a succession of empires, with special attention to the fourth beast who wages war *with its teeth of iron and claws of bronze* until the Ancient of Days (7:22) pronounces judgment and the greatness of the kingdoms are given *to the people of the holy ones of the Most High* (7:27).

In the concluding visions of chapters 8–12, the Hebrew language is once again used. Chapter 8 is dated to the third year of Belshazzar, and here Daniel sees conflict involving a ram and a goat, and sacrilege at the sanctuary (8:13) that must represent the Jerusalem temple. The angel Gabriel is summoned to provide interpretation, with various time references charting the rise and fall of a terrible power that will be broken but not by human hands (8:25). Chapter 9 is dated in the first year of Darius the Mede and features an extended reflection on Jeremiah's prophecy of seventy years through a long prayer of Daniel and another appearance of Gabriel (9:21). Further conflict in envisioned in chapters 10–12, and in the final scenes of the book Daniel is told to keep the book *sealed until the end of time* (12:4), along with a tantalizing hint about resurrection in the last sentence: *But you, go your way and rest; you shall rise for your reward at the end of the days* (12:13, NRSV).

Hour 46: Ezra, Nehemiah

There is early manuscript evidence that the books of Ezra and Nehemiah were originally a single composition, but even when they are divided into two books, a host of shared themes and purposes can be observed. Both books are about the return from exile and various challenges and setbacks when rebuilding the city of Jerusalem—along with the temple—in the aftermath of destruction recorded in 2 Kings 25 and elsewhere. Ezra is a priest and teacher of the law, and during the reign of Artaxerxes he journeys to Jerusalem approximately half a century after the temple is rebuilt. The book of Ezra is structured in two sections: an overview of the time period in chapters 1–6 (4:8–6:18 are written in Aramaic), followed by a first-person memoir in chapters 7–10. The book begins with the edict of Cyrus that formally sets in motion a return to the land:

> *Thus says King Cyrus of Persia: The Lord, the God of heaven, has given me all the kingdoms of the earth, and he has charged me to build him a house at Jerusalem in Judah. Any of those among you who are of his people—may their God be with them!—are now permitted to go up to Jerusalem in Judah, and rebuild the house of the Lord, the God of Israel—he is the God who is in Jerusalem; and let all survivors, in whatever place they reside, be assisted by the people of their place with silver and gold, with goods and with animals, besides freewill offerings for the house of God in Jerusalem.* (Ezra 1:2–4 NRSV)

Prior to Ezra's arrival in Jerusalem that eventually occurs later in the book, the opening chapters are concerned with the return from exile, not so much the journey as the early efforts of restoration. The gifts of gold and silver (1:6) upon their departure from captivity echo the story of Exodus, suggesting that a new journey to the land of promise has commenced. Moreover, the return of the temple vessels taken by Nebuchadnezzar (mockingly used by Belshazzar in Daniel 5:2–4) is highlighted, with the vessels having outlasted the empire that looted them and foreshadowing that the temple from which they were taken will be successfully rebuilt. Chapter 2 provides a long list of those exiles who returned—with Zerubbabel, seen previously in prophetic books, mentioned at the forefront—and at the end of chapter 2 the travelers arrive and many give freewill offerings to start the rebuilding of the temple.

Chapters 3–6 narrate the drama of rebuilding the temple, starting with the altar and then the foundation: *And all the people responded with a great shout when they praised the Lord, because the foundation of the house of the Lord was laid. But many of the priests and Levites and heads of families, old people who had seen the first house on its foundations, wept with a loud voice when they saw this house, though many shouted aloud for joy* (Ezra 3:11–12 NRSV). However, there is opposition among local constituencies in chapter 3, and it continues in chapter 4 with official letters of complaint, to the point that rebuilding work comes to a standstill (4:24). The mention of Haggai and Zechariah in chapter 5 provides a sense of fresh hope—recalling their prophetic activity that we read about earlier—and when King Darius gets involved, there is an imperial decree that results in the completion of the work, crowned with a celebration of the Passover:

> *On the fourteenth day of the first month the returned exiles kept the passover. For both the priests and the Levites had purified themselves; all of them were clean. So they killed the passover lamb for all the returned exiles, for their fellow priests, and for themselves. It was eaten by the people of Israel who had returned from exile, and also by all who had joined them and separated themselves from the pollutions of the nations of the land to worship the Lord, the God of Israel. With joy they celebrated the festival of unleavened bread seven days; for the Lord had made them joyful, and had turned the heart of the king of Assyria to them, so that he aided them in the work on the house of God, the God of Israel.* (Ezra 6:19–22 NRSV)

The arrival of Ezra commences in chapter 7, and it is estimated that between chapters 6 and 7 there is a pause of nearly sixty years. Ezra has an impressive pedigree that is traced back to Aaron, he is devoted to study and observance of the law, and he undertakes the four-month journey from Babylon to Jerusalem. Equipped with a royal letter of authorization from King Artaxerxes, sections of the book now includes the personal perspective of Ezra himself, such as his words at the end of the chapter: *Blessed be the Lord, the God of our ancestors, who put such a thing as this into the heart of the king to glorify the house of the Lord in Jerusalem, and who extended to me steadfast love before the king and his counselors, and before all the king's mighty officers. I took courage, for the hand of the Lord my God was upon me, and I gathered leaders from Israel to go up with me* (Ezra 7:27–28 NRSV). Further details of the personnel and the journey are given in chapter 8, while chapters 9–10 foreground the tense issue of intermarriage. Through a long prayer and lengthy confession of sins, the idea of boundaries moves into view, and the grave risk of assimilation is also raised in the book of Nehemiah that follows.

The first-person perspective in the concluding sections of Ezra continues in Nehemiah, as the book begins with the main character's reminiscences. Occupying a prominent position in the royal court as cupbearer to the king, Nehemiah (whose name means "God has comforted") must be considered an "influencer" in the regime. The main event at the opening of chapter 1 is a report about the status of Jerusalem, as Nehemiah is told: *The survivors there in the province who escaped captivity are in great trouble and shame; the wall of Jerusalem is broken down, and its gates have been destroyed by fire* (Nehemiah 1:3 NRSV). Deeply affected by this situation that he hears about, Nehemiah himself ventures to Jerusalem to participate in the rebuilding, aided by royal sponsorship. Scholars estimate that Nehemiah comes to the city about a dozen years after Ezra, and no doubt his imperial connections, breadth of experience, and leadership skills are vital components in the rebuilding efforts. The central project is the city wall, and there is considerable opposition again from vested local interests. A key moment is Nehemiah's unfiltered prayer in response to the taunts of Tobiah the Ammonite along with Sanballat and the army of Samaria:

> *Hear, O our God, for we are despised; turn their taunt back on their own heads, and give them over as plunder in a land of captivity. Do not cover their guilt, and do not let their sin be blotted out from your sight; for they have hurled insults in the face of the builders.* (Nehemiah 4:4 NRSV)

Amidst adversity and obstacles, the project of the wall is nonetheless completed, and in the process there is concern about the needs of the poor, suggesting a commitment to following the Torah as the city is rebuilt. Ezra the priest makes an appearance in chapter 8 in a celebration with other Levites that includes public reading and feasting: *So they read from the book, from the law of God, with interpretation. They gave the sense, so that the people understood the reading* (Nehemiah 8:8 NRSV). In the concluding chapters the issue of intermarriage again rises to the surface, and Nehemiah's intensity can be seen in his aggressive reaction: *And I contended with them and cursed them and beat some of them and pulled out their hair; and I made them take an oath in the name of God, saying, "You shall not give your daughters to their sons, or take their daughters for your sons or for yourselves." Did not King Solomon of Israel sin on account of such women? Among the many nations there was no king like him, and he was beloved by his God, and God made him king over all Israel; nevertheless, foreign women made even him to sin* (Nehemiah 13:25–26 NRSV). From these concluding scenes, the reader can see the threat to the community's identity. On the one hand, the promises of God are inclusive and will increasingly have a place for the gentiles. On the other hand, at this critical stage there is a stress on purity and the dangers of assimilation. Combined with the spiritual leadership of Ezra, the importance of Nehemiah's contribution to the postexilic community is significant.

Hour 47: 1 Chronicles

THE BOOKS OF 1 and 2 Chronicles are a single literary work, divided into two parts. For readers of English translations such as the NIV and NRSV, Chronicles is located right after 1 and 2 Kings. However, in the Hebrew Bible tradition Chronicles is located in the third section, the Writings, and positioned as the last words of the Hebrew Bible. In terms of chronology, the story is about events prior to Ezra-Nehemiah, but is placed afterwards, perhaps as a "prequel" to that material. First Chronicles begins with the Bible's most extensive genealogy in chapters 1–9, and while it is hard to read, some important themes are established: the eminence of David's line is stressed, and the Jerusalem temple stands at the very center of the earth. After the genealogy, the transition from Saul to David is narrated in chapter 10, ending with the death of Israel's first king at the hands of the neighboring Philistines:

> *They put his weapons in the house of their gods, but his skull they impaled at the house of Dagon. Then all of Jabesh Gilead heard about everything the Philistines did to Saul. So all their men of courage arose, and lifted up the corpse of Saul and the corpses of his sons, and brought them to Jabesh. They buried their bones under the oak tree in Jabesh, and they fasted seven days. Saul died on account of his faithless act, which he did against the Lord, because of the word of the Lord that he did not keep, and also because he asked of a necromancer, to inquire. But he did not inquire of the Lord, and he put him to death. Then the kingdom turned around to David, son of Jesse.* (1 Chronicles 10:10–14)

The remainder of 1 Chronicles is devoted to the reign of David, and while there is considerable overlap with narrative of 1 and 2 Samuel, there is also material not found there. For example, at the end of the installation ceremony when the ark of the covenant is brought to the newly conquered city of Jerusalem, there is a long prayer of David that weaves a number of elements from the Psalms: *Give thanks to the Lord for he is good, his covenant loyalty is eternal. Then say, "Save us, O God of our salvation. Gather us up and rescue us from the nations in order to give thanks to your holy name, to triumph through your praise!" Blessed be the Lord God of Israel from everlasting to everlasting!* (1 Chr. 16:34–36). Another remarkable feature occurs in the census story: when comparing 2 Samuel 24, there is a different character who appears at the very forefront of the narrative:

> *Then Satan stood up against Israel, and he enticed David to number Israel. David said to Joab and the captains of the army, "Go, number Israel from Beersheba to Dan, and come back to me, so I can know the number." Joab said, "May the Lord increase his army 100 times! Are they not, O my lord the king, all of them my lord's servants? Why should he bring guilt to Israel?" But the word of the king was strong against Joab. Then Joab went out and walked around throughout all Israel, and then came back to Jerusalem.* (1 Chronicles 21:1–4)

Toward the end of 1 Chronicles, a vast amount of space is devoted to the preparations for building the temple, in chapters 22–29. Organizing the various personnel is detailed, as well as a vast donation from the king to underwrite the expenses. The centrality of the temple in the Chronicler's story is now evident, and in many respects the book is becoming a virtual biography of the Jerusalem temple. Furthermore, the accession of Solomon, compared to 1 Kings 1–2, is much more peaceful and smooth, suggesting an ideal vision of the past that might operate as a template for the future.

Hour 48: 2 Chronicles

THE FINAL EVENTS OF 1 Chronicles include the transition to Solomon's kingship (*The Lord greatly exalted Solomon in the eyes of all Israel, and placed upon him royal splendor that had not been upon any king in Israel before him*, 1 Chronicles 29:25) and the death of David. Second Chronicles then begins with seamless continuity, and the opening nine chapters highlight the reign of Solomon. A different profile of this controversial king emerges in these pages. While the account in Kings is both a subtle and overt exposition of his several successes and many failures, the Chronicler's account emphasizes his contribution to Israelite history by constructing the Jerusalem temple.

> *So King Solomon was greater than all the kings of the earth in wealth and in wisdom. All the kings of the earth were seeking the presence of Solomon in order to hear his wisdom, that God placed in his mind. Each one of them brought a gift, objects of silver and gold, along with clothing, equipment, spices, horses, and mules, year after year.* (2 Chronicles 9:22–24)

After Solomon's death, the rest of 2 Chronicles narrates the era of the divided kingdom, although there is very little attention to the north and almost exclusive focus on events and reigns of the southern monarchs in Jerusalem. For example, much more attention is given to Rehoboam than Jeroboam, although there is careful mention of the expulsion of Levites from northern territories as they are forced to take refuge in the south. Similarly, there is extended attention to Asa, including his reforms and his problematic final years (*Now the acts of Asa—from beginning to end—are written in the Scroll of the Kings of Judah and Israel. In the thirty-ninth year of his reign Asa became diseased in his feet, severely diseased, but even in his disease he did not seek the Lord, only the physicians. Then Asa lay down with his ancestors, and he died in the forty-first year of his reign. They buried him in his own tomb that he had cut out for himself in the city of David,* 2 Chronicles 16:11–14). Notable exceptions, however, include the attention to the death of Ahab in chapter 18, and a surprising cameo from the prophet Elijah in chapter 21, as he sends a letter to Jehoram of Judah with a frightening warning about the repercussions of his disobedience (*behold, the Lord is about to strike your people, your children, your wives, and all your possessions with a great plague, and you personally will have a major sickness, a disease of your bowels, until your bowels come out, day after day, because of the disease,* 2 Chronicles 21:14–15).

In the aftermath of long reports dedicated to the reign of Hezekiah and the disastrous decisions of Manasseh, the reader may have expected that a comparatively good king like Josiah would receive outstanding press in Chronicles during the final countdown of the southern kingdom in the wake of the Assyrian devastation and incremental advance of Babylon. But while Josiah's reforms are certainly celebrated, his death appears in a more troubling light because he does not heed the wise advice of a foreign king, and instead gets involved in a battle that costs him his life and brings to an early demise an otherwise bright spot in the dismal march toward the end (see 2 Chronicles 35:20–26). The parade of Judah's last monarchs is covered in rapid succession, perhaps to emphasize their incompetence and inability to stem the tide of invasion. The Babylonian attack and Jerusalem's fall are narrated with stunning brevity, and thus the reader's attention falls on the concluding actions of chapter 36. As in the book of Ezra, the decree of Cyrus is quoted as a game-changing moment. As the accent falls on the rebuilding of the ruined temple, the last words of the Hebrew Bible are about the importance of worship and investing in an enduring legacy, believing that God is at work in new and dynamic ways:

> *Now in the first year of Cyrus, king of Persia—to fulfill the word of the Lord spoken through the mouth of Jeremiah—the Lord stirred the spirit of Cyrus, king of Persia, and he released a proclamation throughout all his kingdom and also in writing, saying: Thus says King Cyrus of Persia, "All the kingdoms of the earth have been given to me by the Lord, the God of heaven, and he has appointed me to build him a house in Jerusalem, which is in Judah. Whoever is among you from all his people, may the Lord his God be with him, and let him go up!"* (2 Chronicles 36:22–23)

Afterword

Turning to Matthew

The open-ended invitation to be part of the temple enterprise at the close of 2 Chronicles also affords a good opportunity to glance ahead for those readers interested in forging into the New Testament material. Much could be said, but as a short conclusion to this book, here are few remarks about the book of Matthew, since it would naturally be a good place to continue with the larger storyline. Interesting questions abound as one considers the opening pages of Matthew: what kind of audience is the author primarily addressing, why are there so many interesting characters and events, how does the story of Matthew compare to other books such as Mark and Luke, and how does Matthew's account about Jesus of Nazareth pick up on the major themes and trajectories of the Hebrew Bible? But just to get started, here are seven quick points from chapters 1–4 that draw on some of the discussions in our recent journey through the Law, Prophets, and the Writings.

First, the book of Matthew starts with a genealogy, a genre that is familiar from Genesis, and of course 1 Chronicles 1–9 features the longest genealogical listing of them all. Matthew's initial sentence not only outlines the pedigree of the Messiah, but also announces some of the main contours of the forthcoming plot: *The book of the genesis of Jesus the Messiah, the son of David, the son of Abraham*. Mention of "genesis" (or, origins) takes us back to the creation narrative, and suggests that the arrival of the Messiah signals the possibility of re-creation and a fresh beginning. Moreover, the lineage of Jesus as a descendant of David emphasizes his royal pedigree, and reminds us of the promise to David in 2 Samuel 7 about a son of David forever occupying the throne of Israel. References to Abraham likewise point to the promise of Genesis 12—where every family on earth will be blessed through his offspring—and implies that this promise moves to fruition with the advent of the Messiah. Repeated statements about the deportation to Babylon may also indicate that the arrival of the Messiah represents a deliverance from exile and restoration after captivity.

Second, there are some instantly recognizable names in the genealogy, and the mere mention of figures such as Solomon, Hezekiah, and Manasseh evoke memories of their turbulent royal careers. Female characters such as Tamar, Rahab, and Ruth are also included, and this must point to the inclusion of gentiles in the messianic plan. But altogether this list of names paves the way for the explanation in 1:18–25 of the most important name in the book of Matthew: the angel of God implores Joseph—a descendant of David—to take the pregnant Mary as his wife, for a son has been conceived of the Holy Spirit, *and you will call his name Jesus because he will save his people from their sins.* The name Jesus is the Greek form of Joshua, which means "the Lord is salvation," and so the name foreshadows the story to come (similar to how the name *Moses*, "he who draws out," anticipates the rescue through waters of the Red Sea). Furthermore, another name is included near the end of the chapter, based on the prophetic word of Isaiah 7:15, and *Emmanuel* ("God with us") reveals the abiding presence of Jesus that is highlighted in the last words of the book (28:20).

Third, the visit of the magi at the outset of Matthew 2 provides a reflex to other magician stories: Joseph at the court of Pharaoh in Genesis, for example, and Daniel in Babylon, both of whom triumph over their divinatory antagonists. But there is a reversal here in Matthew, as a mysterious group of magi from the east arrive during the days of King Herod with a startling question: *Where is the one who was born king of the Judeans? For we saw his star at its rising, and have come to worship him.* A foreign king has the last word in Chronicles, and now these foreign magi are the first people to speak in the book of Matthew, since only the angel of the Lord is given direct speech in chapter 1. The guiding star is reminiscent of the guidance of the Israelites through the wilderness (Exodus 23:20), and the image of a rising star is found in the Balaam narrative (Numbers 24:17). Echoes of Isaiah 60 can also be heard (*nations will come to your light . . . they will carry gold and incense, and bring good news of the praises of the Lord*), while the magi's gifts (*gold* for a king, *incense* for a priest, and *myrrh* for burial) variously represent the identity and forthcoming sacrifice of Jesus.

Fourth, there are several references and allusions to Israel's experiences in Egypt. In Matthew 2:13 the angel of God again speaks to Joseph, telling him to take his family and escape from Herod to the land of Egypt. The journey fulfills the prophetic word of Hosea 11:1 (*Out of Egypt I have called my son*) and illustrates how the Messiah is the representative of the people who reenacts the national experiences. As for Herod, when he is outwitted by the magi his fury is unleased in a massacre of the innocents, a grim repetition of Pharaoh's genocidal decree in Exodus 1 with the drowning of the infant males in the waters of the Nile. And yet, in both accounts the tyrannical decree is mitigated by the survival of a child who becomes the agent of rescue. The angel's next speech to Joseph in 2:20 instructs him to leave Egypt because those seeking the child's life are dead, an echo of the words to Moses in Exodus 4:19–20. These allusions collectively signal that a new Exodus is at hand, whereby humanity can be rescued from the evil designs of a tyrant and delivered from slavery to sin. References to Israel's departure from Egypt continue in the next chapters of Matthew's story.

Fifth, at the beginning of Matthew 3 the reader is introduced to the figure of John in the Judean wilderness in the vicinity of the Jordan River. We have to wait until the book of Luke to discover that John has quite an elaborate backstory: he has a miraculous birth, he is from the line of Aaron and therefore should be a priest in temple service, and he is a relative of Jesus on his mother's side because of Mary and Elizabeth's kinship. But John appears in the desert in the prophetic garb of Elijah, and fulfilling the oracle of Isaiah 40 as a herald of the new exodus from captivity. John's opening declaration is *repent* (stressing the need for a change of mind and direction) for *the kingdom of heaven is at hand*, a phrase that occurs over one hundred times in the New Testament, here carrying a sense of urgency because a new divine initiative has been set in motion. John's confrontational rebuke of the Pharisees and Sadducees—religious influencers of the day—includes a reference to *these stones* that probably alludes to the inaugural crossing of the Jordan into the promised land (Deuteronomy 27:4; Joshua 4:7). In his role as forerunner of the Messiah, John insists that someone greater will soon enter the stage, and usher in the era of the Holy Spirit.

Sixth, the event of baptism—a central action of John—at the edge the Jordan River draws crowds from Jerusalem and all over Judea who are confessing their sins. There may well be several purposes for baptism, but most obvious is the parallel with the journey of God's people: just as Israel passed through the waters of Red Sea when they were delivered from Egypt, so baptism signifies the movement from slavery to freedom, from the house of bondage toward the land of promise. There is a problem for

John when Jesus shows up in 3:13–17, but the first words spoken by Jesus insist that his baptism is necessary *to fulfill all righteousness*. Drawing on the rich sacrificial and atonement tradition of the Hebrew Bible (Leviticus 16; Isaiah 53), later New Testament writers affirm that God made *the one who knew no sin to be made sin on our behalf, in order that we might become the righteousness of God in him* (2 Corinthians 5:21), and this gift of righteousness is received by faith (Romans 6:5; Philippians 3:9; Galatians 2:20; see also Hebrews 4:15). When a dove descends in Matthew 3:16 it kindles the memory of the receding floodwaters of chaos in Genesis 8, followed by the divine declaration, *this is my son, whom I love, and with whom I am well pleased* (see Psalm 2:7); by extension the status of being God's child is conferred on all who follow Jesus.

Seventh, when Jesus is led into the wilderness by the Spirit to be tempted by the devil in Matthew 4:1–11, the earlier journey of God's people continues to be retraced as Jesus undergoes a series of trials in an arena of austerity. But the people fail miserably in the narratives of Exodus and Numbers, whereas Jesus does not, and effectively uses the words of Deuteronomy to combat temptations regarding physical needs, spiritual identity, and the use of power. The adversary here has shades of the serpent in the garden of Genesis 3—with several names as well as minions of demonic underlings later in Matthew—and yet these agents of darkness seem to always carry the air of inevitable defeat when they are encountered. There is a gradual upward movement in vv. 1–11, as Jesus travels from the stones on the desert floor, to the pinnacle of the temple, and finally to the top of the highest mountain. It is surely no accident that the book of Matthew ends with Jesus on a mountain in 28:16–20, commissioning the disciples to go forth into all the world. The last words of Jesus in the book—*behold, I am with you every day, even until the end of the age*—reaccentuates the earlier name *Emanuel* taken from Isaiah 7, and highlights the abiding presence and empowerment of the resurrected Messiah with the community of believers.

Only seven short points have been raised here, but there is a great deal more as Matthew continues, with a diverse cast of characters (even the wife of the Roman governor has a cameo appearance) and some remarkable turns in the plot. And indeed, there is lots more in Mark, Luke, and John, each written to different kinds of audiences with a particular angle on the story of Jesus. The book of Luke even has a sequel volume, Acts, featuring a character named Saul of Tarsus, a fierce antagonist of the emerging Jesus movement; yet, in the most spectacular of reversals, the most aggressive and hostile opponent of the Christian faith becomes its most well-traveled and articulate defender as the book of Acts unfolds. This same figure—who is later called Paul—writes a cache of letters, some of which are preserved, and along with some other letters form the rest of the New Testament itself. Climactically, the book of Revelation unveils a powerful and evocative vision of the entire biblical drama from Eden to the new Jerusalem, with hundreds of allusions to stories and prophetic words of the Hebrew Bible. Having invested forty-eight hours in that material during the course of our journey in this book, the reader is much more prepared to understand and appreciate the wealth of the New Testament library.

For Further Reading

THIS SHORT BOOK IS BASED on lecture notes from university and seminary survey courses over the years, and designed as a quick overview of the Hebrew Bible/Old Testament. Because there is a vast quantity of material that was not covered here, the following lineup of twelve items—with twelve being a good biblical number—provide some pointers to the next steps in one's reading adventure. This is just a sample of the many kinds of resources that are available, and a modest attempt to introduce some of the various tools that can be used for more advanced biblical study.

The Hebrew Bible: A Translation with Commentary, 3 volumes, by Robert Alter (New York: W. W. Norton, 2018).

Most biblical translations are done by committees, but this impressive achievement is undertaken by one scholar, with a literary sensitivity and notes that accompany a reading of the entire Hebrew Bible. Here is Alter's rendering of the opening moments: *When God began to create heaven and earth, and the earth then was welter and waste and darkness over the deep and God's breath hovering over the waters, God said, "Let there be light." And there was light.*

The Jewish Study Bible, edited by Adele Berlin and Mark Zvi Brettler (Oxford: Oxford University Press, 2004; second edition, 2014).

Annotations illuminating many aspects of Jewish tradition and the history of interpretation is presented alongside the NJPS translation, and divided into the Torah (Law), Nebi'im (Prophets) and Ketuvim (Writings), the three sections of the Hebrew Bible. This Bible includes introductions to each section and book, and there are numerous essays ranging from "Concepts of Purity in the Bible" to "The Bible in the Dead Sea Scrolls," along with remarks on the calendar and charts with various rulers in biblical times.

The Baker Illustrated Bible Commentary, edited by Gary M. Burge and Andrew E. Hill (Grand Rapids: Baker, 2012).

In a book replete with maps, pictures, and charts, a range of contributors mostly teaching at Christian institutions of higher learning provide accessible commentaries on every book of the Old and New Testaments. Primarily aimed at students, pastors, and small group Bible study leaders, there is also a helpful essay with a historical overview, "What Happened between the Two Testaments?"

The Cambridge Companion to the Hebrew Bible/Old Testament, edited by Stephen B. Chapman and Marvin A. Sweeney (Cambridge: Cambridge University Press, 2016).

According to the cover, "This *Companion* offers a concise and engaging introduction to the Hebrew Bible or Old Testament. Providing an up-to-date snapshot of scholarship, it includes chapters by twenty-three leading scholars specially commissioned for this volume. The volume examines a range of topics, including the historical and religious contexts for the contents of the biblical canon and critical approaches and methods, as well as newer topics such as the Hebrew Bible in Islam, Western art and literature, and contemporary politics."

Introducing the Old Testament: A Historical, Literary, and Theological Survey, by Rolf A. Jacobson and Michael J. Chan (Grand Rapids: Baker Academic, 2023).

Following the typical order of the books found in Christian Bibles, this recent volume provides overviews of each book with charts, sidebars, and helpful discussion of background and context, with dozens of pictures and short forays into various scholarly matters such as "J and P in the Flood Story" and "Prophecy in the Ancient Near East."

The Hebrew Bible as Literature: A Very Short Introduction, by Tod Linafelt (New York: Oxford University Press, 2016).

Featured in a long-running series with hundreds of volumes, this particular book is a concise introduction to the literary qualities of the Hebrew Bible, with a considerable portion dedicated to narrative, while another section deals with poetry. There is also a framing discussion about the seminal influence of the Bible on Western culture.

The New Interpreter's Bible One Volume Commentary, edited by Beverly Roberts Gaventa and David Petersen (Nashville: Abingdon, 2010).

In this condensed version of a mammoth twelve-volume reference work, each biblical book is covered by a diverse team of writers, and general essays on topics such as "How the Bible was Created," "Hebrew Poetry," and the "Culture of Ancient Judaism." Since the volume follows the NRSV, there are also commentaries on the books of the Apocrypha (e.g., Tobit, Judith, 1–4 Maccabees, Bel & the Dragon).

Oxford Bible Atlas, fourth edition, edited by Adrian Curtis (Oxford: Oxford University Press, 2007).

Replete with maps and geographical resources, including a rare photo of Jerusalem covered in snow, this volume also includes succinct surveys of major historical events such as the rise of Assyria, and the battles of the Babylonians. Conveys a sense of the landscape of biblical places and surrounding nations from the settings of the Genesis narratives and era of the Israelite kingdoms, through the Persian period and the conquests of Alexander, and into the Hellenistic age of the New Testament and the Roman empire.

The Epic of Eden: A Christian Entry into the Old Testament, by Sandra L. Richter (Downers Grove, IL: InterVarsity, 2008).

In this popular introduction that starts with an image of a dysfunctional closet as way of describing many people's experience of the Hebrew Bible, the author then starts with a plan to reorganize things with some easy-to-understand chapters on the concept of covenant, Moses and the tabernacle, and David and the monarchy, as part of a larger argument of the Bible as a story of redemption.

Reading the Old Testament as Christian Scripture, by Mark S. Gignilliat and Heath A. Thomas (Grand Rapids: Baker Academic, 2025).

"The entire *history* of Israel was useless: away with it!" This quote from Friedrich Nietzsche is cited at the start of this introductory textbook, and armed with discussion questions, pictures of famous artwork, and diagrams, the authors aim to provide a constructive response to Nietzsche's claim. Using the order of the books in the Hebrew Bible and addressing various academic issues along the way, this volume provides a survey of biblical theology for a primarily Christian audience.

The Old Testament is Dying: A Diagnosis and Recommended Treatment, by Brent A. Strawn (Grand Rapids: Baker Academic, 2017).

"Drawing on the analogy of a dying language," says one of the endorsers of this book, "Strawn brings his encyclopedic mind and seemingly limitless creativity to bear on the problem of the silence of the Old Testament in the church today. The diagnosis is daunting, but the prognosis, if followed, is hopeful. This important book promises to breathe life into the church's attempts to speak God's truth today, especially for those who still find the *viva vox* [living voice] of the gospel in the Old Testament."

Anchor Bible Dictionary, edited by David Noel Freedman, 6 vols. (New York: Doubleday, 1992).

Not for the faint of heart, this is a weighty resource with entries on every conceivable topic ranging from Aaron, Abaddon, and Abigail, all the way to Zadok, Zeruiah, and Zuph. Some critics might demur that *ABD* is a bit dated—and to be sure, there are no references to YouTube—but it is still an impressive repository that can be used profitably alongside more recent works such as the *Encyclopedia of the Bible and Its Reception* or the Society of Biblical Literature's online *Bible Odyssey* project.

www.ingramcontent.com/pod-product-compliance
Lightning Source LLC
LaVergne TN
LVHW090520110826
845146LV00003B/930
* 9 7 9 8 3 8 5 2 3 6 8 1 7 *